SAND PILOT OF MORECAMBE BAY

Official Guide over the Kent Sands

Cedric Robinson

With line drawings by Olive Robinson

DAVID & CHARLES
NEWTON ABBOT LONDON NORTH POMFRET (Vt)

To my parents, and my wife Olive

British Library Cataloguing in Publication Data

Robinson, Cedric
Sand pilot of Morecambe Bay
1. Morecambe Bay region, Eng. - Social life and customs
I. Title
942.7'83 DA670.M/

ISBN 0-7153-7915-1

Typeset by Photoprint, Paignton and printed in Great Britain by
A. Wheaton & Co. Ltd. Exeter Devon
for David & Charles (Publishers) Limited
Brunel House Newton Abbot Devon

Published in the United States of America
by David & Charles Inc
North Pomfret Vermont 05053 USA

Contents

Foreword

by Hugh Cavendish
Trustee, Guides over the Sands

In this book, Cedric Robinson unveils the secrets of his moody, treacherous and outstandingly beautiful lifetime companion, Morecambe Bay, and its Sands.

In one sense, this is a cautionary tale dedicated to those who overlook the registers and silent graves, at Cartmel Priory and elsewhere, which bear witness to the fate of those who chose not to show proper respect for the Sands in bygone centuries. In another sense, it is a story of endurance and adventure; of a tradition of hardy fishermen and their families who, in partnership with their unique environment, have made the Sands a way and a means of life — a sort of seafaring life without boats.

It is a vivid personal account. Mr. Robinson is not an historian, yet he writes with a deep sense of history: for what is it but living history when he describes his work as an official guide — a post created by ancient charter — taking travellers across the Sands?

Brought up on the shores of Morecambe Bay, all my life I have walked and ridden on its sands and swum in its channels. I have taken risks and come close to suffering the consequences. As long as I live, I believe I will always be strongly attracted by the magic, power and beauty of the Sands, but I also know that I will never gain that intimacy which is reserved for those to whom they are a life and a livelihood.

This tidal coast has brought at times prosperity, at times lean years; it has sustained and claimed human life and it has given great pleasure as well as some sorrow. One highly pleasing aspect of this account is that while Cedric Robinson accepts that much has changed and much has gone forever in the life of the Sands, he knows that they still have a future. No one can foresee with any accuracy what the future holds for Morecambe Bay in terms of the harvest it may yield. Two things, however, are certain: it will continue to charm and beckon those who set eyes on it, and there will always be a need for men like Cedric Robinson to be trustees of its secrets and unpredictable ways.

His book is proof that an understanding and a knowledge of the Sands, though within the gift of only a very few, have a value which will endure so long as the tide ebbs and flows in Morecambe Bay.

Holker Hall
Cark-in-Cartmel
August 1979

PART ONE
FOLLOWING THE SANDS

1 Early Days in Flookburgh

For hundreds of years, before the coming of the Furness Railway in 1857, the journey from Lancaster to Ulverston and beyond was over the sands of Morecambe Bay, and across both the Kent and the Leven estuaries. Many a harrowing tale has been told in the past of the 'over sands' route. Coaches with their horses and passengers were lost in the treacherous quicksands, and the churchyard at Cartmel Priory has many graves of those who were drowned while trying to cross the estuaries.

It was not only travellers who faced the hazards of the bay. Every day fishermen from the villages on the coast went out with their horses and carts to catch the shrimps and cockles and other fish which were their main livelihood. It was a dangerous way of earning a living, and depended upon the knowledge of the sands which was handed down from one generation to the next.

Here you will read of the village of Flookburgh, on the west coast of the Cartmel peninsula, and of a Flookburgh family who still go out to earn a living 'following the sands'.

A stranger to Flookburgh some forty years ago might have looked with surprise at a small boy of five or six years, in wellington boots several sizes too big for him, urging an unwilling billygoat, harnessed to a wooden box on a couple of old pram wheels, through the beck which ran alongside the village street. The goat was loath to get his feet wet, and in the way of goats, turned his horns on the boy who, quite unafraid of the goat's antics, grabbed Billy by the rope bridle and the near-side horn and half led, half dragged the unco-operative animal through the shallow water. Picking up some empty cockle shells which had been thrown into the beck, he loaded them into the cart and took them promptly home to his mother.

The small boy, Cedric Robinson, known to all the local people as Ced, was doing what most small boys do — copying his father, who, that morning as on most days, summer and winter, had gone out on to the changing sands of the bay to gather cockles.

In all too short a time this play was to become reality, and young Cedric had to join his father in the hard task of winning a living from the sea and sands of Morecambe Bay.

All this was more than forty years ago, and now the mature Cedric will take over the telling of this story.

My father was born in Flookburgh in 1904 and spent most of his life as a fisherman and fish salesman. For about two years, after leaving school, he was hired out into farm service at a wage of five pounds for six months; but even then the sea had an influence on his life. He worked at East Plain Farm, Flookburgh. That's down the mile road, which runs from the village to the sea, down on the flat ground where the aerodrome was built during the war. In Dad's young days, Harry Tyson had that farm. Being so close to the shore, it was exposed to the severe weather of the bay. When the gales came, there was no warning on the radio as there would be today.

One time, there was a terrific gale, which went on day after day, and eventually the sea broke through the embankment. Dad had been out with the milk in the morning, and came back to find his boss taking his shoes off; he said he was wet through. He had been down on to the lowland, Broadwater, as they called it. Here the sea was washing over the embankment, and it had also made a big hole through the banking. There was no give in the weather, so all the animals were moved off the farm to other farms on higher ground. They were taken to West Plain Farm and to another, called Mire Side, right up the village of Flookburgh. All the household furniture and carpets were carried upstairs. For two or three days the gale raged. When eventually it was possible to go back, after it had calmed down, they found that the tide had been up the roads and up the dykes, the sea had left brods — that is, all the sticks and stuff that is carried in on the tide — around the dykes, and had just reached the farmhouse, though it hadn't gone inside. The banking had to be repaired after the storm, and thorns cut from hedges and placed all along the embankment to prevent the sheep from making permament paths through it. These had to be renewed regularly, especially at high tides, until more lasting repairs could be made.

After leaving the farm, Dad went out with his father on to the sands to help to get the cockles, mussels and wet fish which provided the family with a living. He had three brothers and three sisters. The girls all went into domestic service at Grange-over-Sands after they left school, as there was little else in the way of work at that time. One of them, Marie, eventually owned the village post office for a number of years.

Dad has spent most of his life working in and around Morecambe Bay, as his father did before him, and he knows the changing sands like the back of his hand, as they say. He can tell where the different dykes and channels will be, after the next tide, by the way the wind is blowing, the direction from which it is coming and the way the rivers are running. There are three rivers emptying into the east side of Morecambe Bay. The main one is the Kent, which comes in under the Arnside viaduct. The Winster is on the Grange-over-Sands side, and the Keer enters the bay near Carnforth. The bay is far more treacherous when there has been heavy rain, bringing a great weight of fresh water from the hills all around. In this area of the Cartmel peninsula there are a great many freshwater springs; some of these find their way right out into the bay and bubble up through the sand some distance from the shore. Such places are very dangerous and you would go down like a stone if you got into one of these spots. Dad learnt all this from his father and through years of experience out there on his own.

Mam was born at Glasson Dock, a small village port near Lancaster, in 1912, and after leaving school, where she made quite an impression in the art class (there are still some drawings of hers hanging up in the school), she went to work as a barmaid at the Stork Hotel at Condor Green, near Lancaster. Her father was a dock labourer and her mother worked in a sawmill.

When they were first married my parents lived at Hambleton, near Poulton-le-Fylde, a small village alongside the River Wyre. Father went musselling, fluking and catching codling to make a living. As the river ran close to the shore, fishing in that area was easy to hand. The mussells were of good quality, near to the side of the river, on what we called scars or skeers. These scars have a hard foundation of small rocks, sand and stone, which is ideal for masses of young mussels to live and grow upon. Although in that area there was not a vast quantity, the quality made the job worthwhile.

The mussel fork used for gathering them had two straight metal prongs about 3 to 4in long and a wooden handle just long enough to be gripped by the fingers. The back of the hand came into contact with the rocks as each mussel was prized from its bed, so it had to be well bandaged to protect the knuckles from being grazed. When enough mussels had been gathered together over a few days in the cool wintry weather, Father would get a contractor to take them over Shard bridge, a toll bridge which crossed the River Wyre, and on to Poulton station. From there, they went into Lancashire towns.

When the tides were not suitable for musselling, my father would set his nets to catch codling. For this, he used what we call the bag or stake net, the same kind of net as is used for catching flukes to this day. After each tide, he went round the streets hawking his catch.

As time went on, the mussel beds were condemned by the fishing authorities, so he turned his hand to peat cutting on Pilling Marshes for 7s 6d (37½p) a day. He also went on to the farms, muck-spreading, which was all done by fork in hand in those days. But fishing was what he knew and loved, and as my parents could see no future in fishing around Hambleton area, they decided to move back to Father's native village of

Flookburgh, where his mother, brothers and sisters still lived. They managed to get furnished rooms with a Mr and Mrs Tyson, at Hill Foot, until such time as a very small cottage became available in the centre of the village — No 4, Market Cross. It was here that my younger sister Jean and I were born; my other sister Peggy had been born in Hambleton. The really strange thing about it, though, was that my Father himself had been born in the very same house, back in 1904. Some years after the move, while Father was serving overseas with the Eighth Army during the war, the row of cottages came up for sale, but Mother, not quite knowing what to do in his absence, missed the chance of buying the one we occupied. They were sold for £80 each; today, similar cottages in the village, with a little modernisation, are fetching around £10,000.

It was not very easy for my Mother to cope with us youngsters in such a small cottage without any modern conveniences. The rooms were very small, just a living room and a tiny kitchen downstairs, with two bedrooms upstairs. There was no water laid on, and a tap in the yard was shared by the people living in the five adjoining cottages, as was the old earth closet, which was about a hundred yards away. All water for use in the house was brought in in buckets, and a bucket full of clean water always stood on the table in the back kitchen. At this stage there was no electricity either: candles were used for lighting, and meals were cooked on the coal fire. We had a big tin bath which was brought in from the peat-house on bath night, the water having to be heated over the fire in pans and kettles. The rent for the cottage was 5s (25p) a week.

The village primary school was only a short distance from our cottage. It had only two rooms, and an adjoining wooden building was used as a classroom for the very young; the main attraction there was a large wooden rocking horse. I did not like school at first, and whenever the opportunity came along I would run home and hide under the kitchen table, pulling the red chenille cloth well down to one side so as not to be seen. But here the teacher would find me, dragging me out and spanking me and carrying me back to school like a sack of potatoes. Oddly enough, despite this bad start I came to like her more and more, and as I settled down I became a favourite with her too.

I remember at Christmas, in our second year when we had moved into the main school building, being asked to write lists of things we would most like to have for Christmas. These the teacher posted up the chimney of the very large fireplace, leaning carefully over the high fireguard which was always in place around the roaring fire. A short while later we were all taken round to the yard at the back of the school, and there to our delight found Father Christmas waiting with a huge Christmas tree and a sack of toys. The tree was taken into the school and erected, while we children gazed out of the windows and up into the clouds, hoping to catch a glimpse of Father Christmas departing with his reindeer.

At the age of ten I moved on to the Holker Church of England school, which was a two-mile walk from Flookburgh. Although by now I had become pretty good at school work, it was animals that were always at the forefront of my mind. I wasn't really keen on sport, but wherever there was a horse, there I would be. They drew me then, as they do to this day. In those days they usually threw me too!

There was a riding and racing stable near to the school, owned at that time by a Mr George Dickinson, and there my mates and I spent all our spare time. I remember coming from church one Sunday evening, soon after I had had my first suit with long trousers. I went straight to the stables to have a ride, and as I urged the horse to gallop up the lane, he threw me off right in a muddy gateway. For what seemed an age I didn't dare to go home. When I eventually plucked up the courage to return, I got a terrible hiding — but it didn't stop me from going back to the stables the very next day!

I joined the village band at quite an early age, playing the trombone, and was also in the choir for seven years at the church my parents attended, St John's Flookburgh, where, appropriately, there is a fish instead of the usual cock on the weather vane. I still have my trombone, though I don't get time to play it much these days, but I sing all the time when I am out on the sands on my own. The birds don't seem to mind!

My very first experience of fishing with a horse and cart on Morecambe Bay was when a local fisherman took me out with him one day, when he was going to fish his fluke nets. He had no fear at all, and was well known for this throughout the village. He was going out from Humphrey Head, where the river channel cut in and was quite deep. This fisherman put me up on his cart, and as I was only then a bit of a nipper I can't remember whether anyone knew where I was. Anyway, he struck in with his horse through Holy Well Dyke, until the horse had to swim because of the depth of the water. There were several boxes and a basket or two in the cart; the water got so deep and so cold — I remember it just as if it were happening now! The man picked me up and stood me on the fore-end of his cart, but the water was still rising, and you know how when cold water comes up your belly, it takes your breath away and you can't get your wind. I was gasping for breath, and thought my end had come.

Now the fisherman had a very good, quiet horse, which he called Eggy, because he had got him off a fellow from over the other side of the bay who was nicknamed Eggy. He used that horse for many years. Well, Eggy turned round and swam back to the shore; we lost some floorboards from the cart on the way, so it must have been an old one. The man lost his cockle baskets, he lost his boxes, he lost almost everything. When we reached the side, there was a chap on the shore with a wagon, getting water from the Holy Well. They used to sell the water in those days, and I have since learnt that it was believed to have medicinal properties. This chap lifted me out of the cart and sat me in his wagon, dripping wet. He took me home, and I have never forgotten how I felt. The next day, the fisherman told Dad all about it. He said he had simply waited until Eggy had rested a while, then gone on to fish his fluke nets.

I wasn't very much older, about six or seven I should think, when Dad heard about a horse which was for sale at Ulverston. A horse dealer had bought four from a firm that was giving up horses and going in for motor transport. We went through on the train, as we had no means of transport in those days. The horse was away up on the fells, so we trudged up there and brought him down to the dealer's yard. Dad gave him a good looking over and decided to buy him.

'Is he a quiet 'un?' Dad asked.

'Oh aye, mi lad,' said the dealer.

'Do yer think t'lad'll be aw reet on his back then?'

'Aye,' he said.

Well, they put me up on him and he went right up in the air and chucked me off! Dad's plan was to walk the horse home to save the cost of putting him on the train. This would have been a good idea if I could have ridden on him, and Dad would have walked alongside holding the bridle. It was about twelve to fourteen miles from Ulverston to Flookburgh, and by gum! I was tired for a month after that journey. He proved to be a good little horse though, and we kept him for some time, then bought a bigger one which could go into deeper water. The horse did some good work too, for the fisherman who bought him from Dad, but he wouldn't have anyone on his back at any price.

I started while still at school to follow the sands with my Dad, whose main job in those days was gathering cockles for the markets of the nearby towns of Lancashire and Yorkshire. He went out, wet or fine, summer and winter, as a living was hard to get at that time, and there were five of us and the horse to be kept. I could only go in the school holidays and at weekends, but on some days, if Dad had a big order for several bags of cockles which had to be sent off by train, my two sisters would also come with us. They were a good help and were soon very quick at the job. We had some very good customers in the towns, and they knew they could depend on us too, so we would set out, whatever the weather, to fulfil our orders.

We fishermen have to live our lives according to the tides. The tide tells you what time you must get up in the morning, what time you can get your meals and when you can go to bed at night. Many a time we had to be up before daylight, when I would take water out to the stable for the horse and my sisters would each take him an armful of hay, so that he was fed and watered in good time before we had to harness him to the cart. We then loaded everything we would be likely to need onto the cart. First came the jumbo. This is a thick plank of hardwood about 4ft 6in long and 18in wide. It has two long handles fastened to the upper side and it is rocked to and fro on the wet sand until the cockles show on the surface; then you step back and work on the next strip of sand, while the others follow with the cramb, a tool we have made for us by the local blacksmith. It is about 14in long, and has three tempered metal prongs, like a curved fork. It makes the job much easier than would be the case if you had to pick each cockle up by hand. It saved us a lot of backache, and soon filled our baskets. We also took a riddle, to sort out the very small shellfish so that they could grow on for the next season; three or four baskets and some hessian sacks, which we hoped to bring back full of big juicy cockles, a sack of hay and some oats for the horse, and a very warm rug to throw over him to keep him comfortable while we worked. He would have to be fastened to a stake, which Dad would drive well into the sand behind the cart, which was tipped up with its shafts in the air when we had unyoked the horse. This made a bit of a windbreak as it could be bitterly cold out there. However good a horse you might have, he has to be well tethered or he may wander off and you would be left out there with all your gear.

Our very lives depended on our horse, and we looked after him carefully. Although the horses were worked hard, they were always well fed and there was never a poor one to be seen on the sands. Some people thought it was cruel when they saw horses pulling the carts through the water, sometimes well up to their bellies, but the sea water did them good; the racehorse trainers have found this out, and they often take their horses for a chase along the sands and a dip in the sea.

In Dad's younger days, most fisherfolk in Flookburgh had large families, and they all followed the sands in winter time, helping to gather the cockles. Jumbos were used all the year round, until new bye-laws were introduced which made it illegal for the fishermen to use them in the summer. It was thought that these restrictions would help to preserve the immature shellfish. Many of the smaller cockles were getting broken by the use of the jumbo, and as the small ones were all left behind they were eaten up by the sea birds.

An experienced fisherman could still gather the cockles in summer by using the cramb and striking the cockles one at a time from under the sand. His practised eye looked for the two minute holes which showed on the drier patches of sand, betraying the presence of the cockle beneath. In wetter areas, a small moss identified the spot. This method was called groating and mossing but was naturally not so popular with the fishermen, and in time families began to break the law.

Wooden boards were hidden in the cart on the outward journey, and on arrival at the cockling grounds were tied to the youngsters' feet. Keeping together and tramping up and down, they made the sands move and the cockles come up to the surface, just as the jumbo did. The tail-board of the cart was also used, but as it had no handles a rope was fastened so that the fishermen could rock it to and fro and then move it on. Where there's a will, they say, there's a way, and a little imagination is a great help in the important task of making a living.

Just after the war, when Dad came home from the army, he fitted himself out with all the gear he would need to start up fishing again. We had a grand horse, and in a bit of a field not far from the back of our cottage were the stables. We had two in the middle of a row of six, with our horse Daisy in one, and the store of hay for the winter feed in the other. There was an old horse in the next stable and on the other side of ours were two horses belonging to a neighbour. All Dad's gear, except the cart and his sea boots, were kept in the stable, and along the back were the newly tarred nets. In those days the nets were not treated with preservative as they are today, so we had to tar them before use and hang them up to dry.

Sadly, it was not long before disaster struck. We always went to bed in good time, ready to make an early start next morning. So we were already in bed when we were alarmed at about ten-thirty one evening by shouting and commotion outside. Looking out of the window, we saw a fierce red glow in the night sky. We all grabbed a few clothes and dashed outside. The stables, built of wood, were ablaze. Horses were neighing and stamping, people were screaming and shouting, and black smoke billowed up into the sky.

Dad tried to get near enough to look through the window of our stable but could see nothing of our Daisy. We thought she had gone down in the fire, and it was heartbreaking to think of losing his horse. The old horse in the next stable was lying motionless on the floor. He was a gonner. The other two were still in their stable and several people were hacking away at the burning wood of the door with anything they could find: spades, axes, iron bars. It seemed that all the villagers were there carrying buckets of water in a vain effort to stem the fire. The tarred nets and the bales of hay fed the flames and it seemed impossible that any animal could still be alive. Then, the man who owned one of the trapped horses broke into the burning stables and, although the smoke was so thick inside, managed to free the two animals.

Next someone down at the watering spot shouted, 'There's a horse over here!' It was our Daisy! She must have broken her rope and smashed her way out at the back of the stable, but with the smoke so thick, no one had seen her run away. What a relief that was to all of us. Everything else had gone up in the flames: cockle baskets, nets, stakes, oilskins, all the winter's feed, all lost. Mum and Dad were almost in tears, but when we found Daisy was safe, at least we had something to start with again. In her struggle to free herself from the rope which held her, Daisy had strained her neck, and afterwards she used to shake her head at times. But she was a wonderful horse; we had her for many years.

It was a miracle that any of the horses got out alive. The old one which had died in the fire had been fastened with a heavy chain and a strong leather halter and so had no chance of breaking out. The fisherman who risked his life to save the two trapped animals later received an award for his bravery, which everyone in the village felt he certainly deserved.

We were lucky that the watering place for the horses was a freshwater spring and that it was only about twenty yards away from the stables, as there was no time to get a fire engine out and anyway there wasn't a telephone within reach. In those days, few people could afford to have a phone in the house. The fire came after a hot, dry summer and there was everything there to feed it. We never did find out how the fire started: some people thought that a carelessly thrown cigarette end among newly tarred nets had caused the blaze, but we shall never know.

The following morning we were able to see the full extent of the damage. The charred remains of the old horse lay among the burnt-out stables, with bits of netting and shrivelled pieces of Dad's oilskins. It was a terrible loss for us all, but we still had our living to earn, and we soon put all our efforts into getting the gear together once more, ready for work.

One cold morning, we set out from Flookburgh with several other fishermen, all making for the cockling grounds across the bay, with Dad in the lead. 'We'll have to go round Betty Lawrence Dyke this morning, as last night's tide will have left a deep channel near in to the Headland.' It was so cold sitting on the cart that we children would rather run behind to keep ourselves warm. Sometimes we would hang on to the tailboard, letting go when our hands got too cold to hold on. 'Mind you keep near in to t'cart, you young 'uns,' Dad shouted. 'There's a few soft spots round 'ere.' Betty Lawrence Dyke is fresh water, and this is always dangerous.

It was a long weary journey for us, and we should have been frozen through sitting for so long on the cart. The way seemed never-ending. 'Not much farther now. Keep near the cart; it's getting a bit of a mist about here, but it'll soon clear.' Dad had to keep his eye on us all the time, as we could be in trouble if we strayed even a few yards from the track he was taking.

By now all sight of the land was lost in the whirling wisps of the misty morning. I always looked forward to going out on the sands; it was like being in a different world out there. 'Are we nearly there now?' one after the other would ask. Dad pointed ahead. 'Yon marker, can you see it?' At last we had reached the good spot we had worked on the day before, where Dad had put a short stake in the sand to enable us to find the place more easily. These markers were short branches pushed deep into the sand. They would stay for quite a long time if the tides were not too rough. Our old Christmas tree was put in for a marker out in the middle of the bay, and stayed there for weeks on end. It looked as if it was growing, until the salt water killed off all the needles. You couldn't use anything like iron bars or such, as they would be a danger to boats or to nets when the tide covered them.

We found the cockles were 'rank' — that is to say they were very plentiful — and we soon unyoked the horse. Dad fastened him up to the stake behind the cart, which was quickly unloaded. Then he got busy with the jumbo and we three youngsters were soon flicking the cockles into the baskets with our crambs. As soon as a basket was full, Dad would empty the cockles into a sack. The sacks were then put near the cart and we would work on, sometimes for four or five hours at a stretch. It was hard work, but we couldn't rest, as the shellfish would burrow into the sand again if we were too slow in picking them up, and we had to get all we could before the tide came, leaving ourselves just time to get back across the bay. At last we had filled all the sacks, so Dad and I yoked up the horse and loaded the sacks and all the gear on the cart. 'We shall have to get a move on now. Look yer, coming in misty again.' With that, we climbed into the cart. There was just room for the girls, amongst the bags of cockles, and I sat at the fore-end with Dad.

We were soon well out into the bay, going along at a good trot, when suddenly the horse reared and almost threw me off. Dad reined him in and, looking round, we could see coming out of the mist a huge stag. It ran almost up to the horse and then turned back and forth across our path. We waited to see what it would do. It seemed half crazed, poor thing. Dad said it would have taken to the water somewhere up the coast, to avoid hunters, and probably been swimming for some time, until it came to the north end of the bay. We let it get ahead before we started off again along our tracks, hoping it would soon reach the shore and get away to safety. It was a magnificent creature, and this was the first time I had seen one so far out in the bay. We were all saddened to hear, a few days later, that the stag had been shot by a fisherman as it came on to the land; but no doubt a number of families were glad to have venison for their Sunday dinner.

2 Harvest of the Sands

For many of the families in the bay, including our own, cockle fishing was a main source of livelihood. Because of this, we were always on the lookout for new and more profitable grounds. For a number of years the cockles on the Flookburgh sands, though large and of a very good quality, had been spread thinly over a large area. So in 1946 Dad and another Flookburgh fisherman decided to cross the sands to Silverdale, and then on to Hest Bank, having heard rumours of a cockle bed over there.

It was very exciting, getting ready to go out to these new grounds. We would have to take large quantities of everything as long as it would all fit in the cart: jumbo, crambs, cockle baskets, riddle and, on this occasion, a drag, which is like a garden rake, but very strong. This was a sign that we were expecting the cockles to be plentiful, as this was the only time the drag was used. We also needed something for the horse — a bale of hay and a bag of oats, as it was winter time. That would last him for a few days. Then something for ourselves — sandwiches and flasks — and we were ready for off, Dad and me with our cart and the other fisherman with his. We met at Flookburgh Square and off we set. What excitement and experience I was to get from all this.

We made our way first to Allithwaite, then up Jack Hill, of all places! I thought the horses with their heavily loaded carts would never make it up the steep hill, which must be about one in three. Eventually we did reach the top, and away we went through Kents Bank and down Carter Road — another steep hill, but this time we were going down! We crossed the railway by the level crossing, and took the slipway down on to the sands, which hereabout were often very muddy, there being a freshwater spring near by. Coming to the channel of the River Kent, near to the shore, we must have been a bit late on the tide, as it was very deep crossing. The horses just made it, half swimming, only touching bottom now and then. Once we were out of the water we had a look at the tackle on the carts. Most of it had got wet but the fodder for the horses was dry, so we set off at a good pace for Silverdale, where we knew a farmer with whom we had arranged to stable the horses. The route took us over five miles or so of fairly firm sand, and we made good going. On arrival we unhitched the carts, fed, watered and stabled our horses, and then, having had a bite and a drink ourselves, set off on the long walk to Silverdale station to get on the train for home, where we knew there would be a hot meal waiting to warm us up.

The following day we took the train from Cark station, near Flookburgh, back to Silverdale and walked to the farm to feed and water the horses; then we harnessed them to the carts, which we loaded with everything we had brought over the sands the day before. At the turn of the tide, we were off out of the farmyard, down to the shore and across the marsh over the sands to the cockling grounds. When we arrived, I wondered what we should do with any cockles we got, as the carts were already loaded, but soon everything was put on to one cart. Seemingly, this first day was only to look around and get our bearings, and to find the best places. Although we found the cockles very good, Dad and his mate thought there would be even better beds up nearer to Hest Bank, where, true enough, they were really rank. There were already two fishermen, locals, who fished this stretch of sand for cockles, so we kept our distance.

Hest Bank was to become almost a second home to us for the next two years. We had stabling for the horses and could leave our carts and all our tackle there at the farm, so we were able to make cockling our chief source of income. For a while, we were the only men from Flookburgh to go over the bay, but in time the word passed through the village; more and more families of fishermen came to join us, and they too had to find stabling for their horses.

At Hest Bank, we were getting cockles as fast as we could pick them up, but after a while as we moved on we found the sand getting harder and harder. Being the lad, I had to follow the first jumbo with a second one in an attempt to soften the

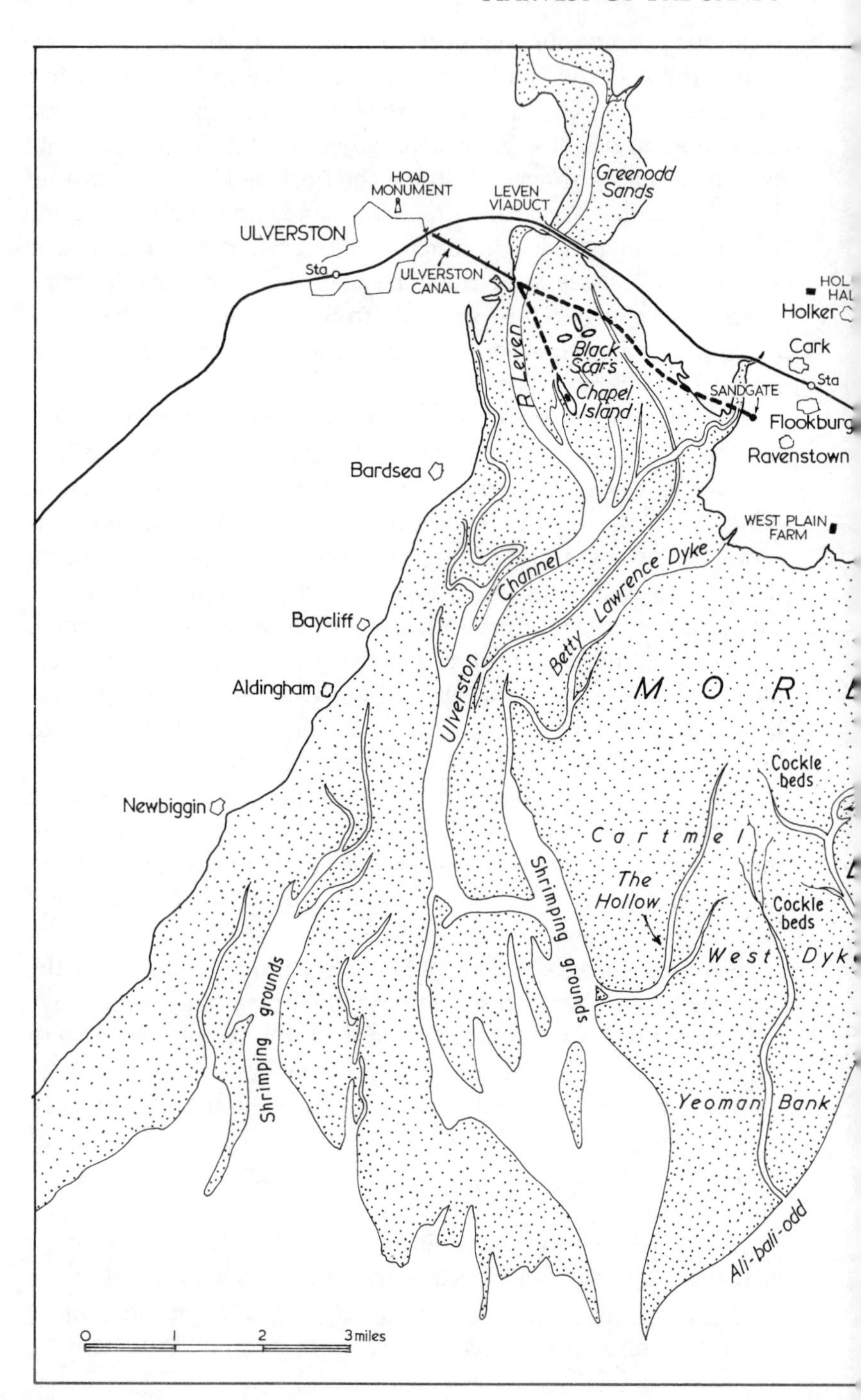

HOAD MONUMENT
LEVEN VIADUCT
Greenodd Sands
ULVERSTON
Sta
ULVERSTON CANAL
Holker
Cark
Sta
R. Leven
Black Scars
Chapel Island
SANDGATE
Flookburg
Ravenstown
Bardsea
WEST PLAIN FARM
Channel
Betty Lawrence Dyke
Baycliff
Aldingham
Ulverston
M O R
Cockle beds
Newbiggin
Cartmel
The Hollow
Cockle beds
Shrimping grounds
West Dyk
Shrimping grounds
Yeoman Bank
Ali-bali-odd
0 1 2 3 miles

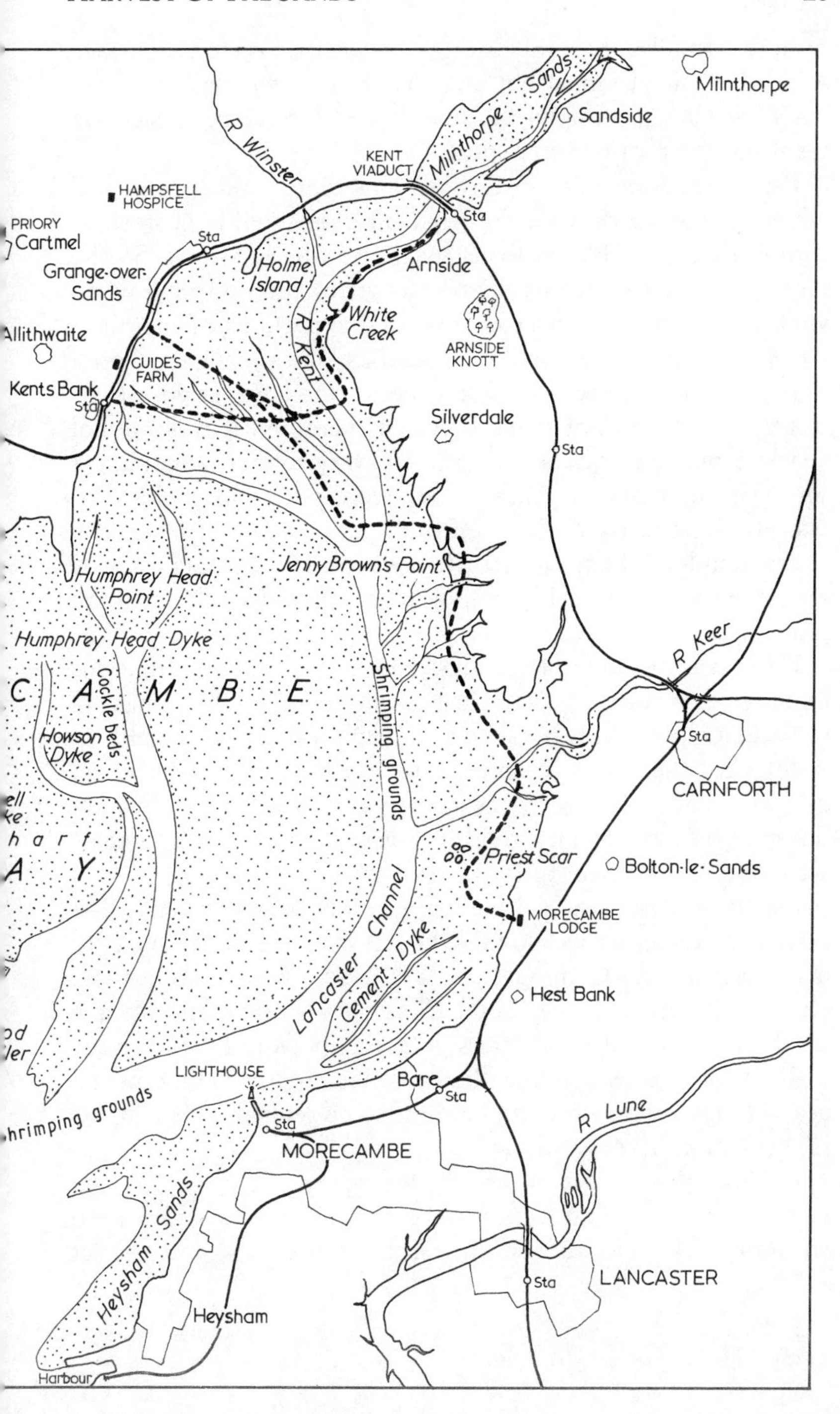
Milnthorpe
Sandside
Milnthorpe Sands
R Winster
KENT VIADUCT
Sta
HAMPSFELL HOSPICE
PRIORY
Cartmel
Grange-over-Sands
Holme Island
Arnside
White Creek
R Kent
ARNSIDE KNOTT
Allithwaite
GUIDE'S FARM
Kents Bank
Silverdale
Humphrey Head Point
Jenny Brown's Point
Humphrey Head Dyke
Cockle beds
C A M B E
Shrimping grounds
R Keer
Howson Dyke
CARNFORTH
Priest Scar
Bolton-le-Sands
Lancaster Channel
Cement Dyke
MORECAMBE LODGE
Hest Bank
LIGHTHOUSE
Bare
hrimping grounds
R Lune
MORECAMBE
Heysham Sands
LANCASTER
Heysham
Harbour

ground. Usually, the jumbo brings the shellfish up to the surface in a very short time, but this patch was so hard that we christened it 'Cement Dyke'! Then, as it didn't get any easier, we went in search of a better spot.

We worked steadily on through the winter and spring, and when summer came, we were often entertained with music from Morecambe pier, blown to us by the southerly winds. So the days passed pleasantly enough, except for the odd time when we found ourselves a bit too close to one particular fisherman. He was a rather aggressive type, and as Dad's mate also had a fiery temper, they would have been at one another with their drags if Dad had not come between them. As it was, verbal sparks would fly and then we moved away so that we could get on with our work in peace. There were plenty of cockles for everybody. We would load up one cart and take it off to the shore to unload them, so that when we found the tide chasing us we hadn't so much tackle to look to and could work on to the last minute.

Hest Bank station porters must have wondered what had hit them. Horses and carts with their load of cockles, the siding full of wagons laden with bags, each holding a hundredweight . . . cockles for the towns of Lancashire and Yorkshire, who were, as I have said, our biggest customers in those days. It is quite different today, when it would cost as much to dispatch them as we could expect them to fetch.

On the occasions when we went home for a night and had missed the train, we would take the bus from Carnforth, usually a double-decker. Coming from a village where all the buses were single-deckers, we found these very strange and always tried to get a seat downstairs. One chap would rather have walked all the way home than go upstairs. When someone asked him why he wouldn't go on top, he replied quite simply, 'Theer's nah driver up theer.'

In time, the cockles became rather scarce. Some of the men got unsettled and, as spring came again, a few of them tried shrimping at Flookburgh. Dad and I still had a good order

The Morecambe Bay area, showing the various fishing grounds and the routes of the cross-bay walks (dotted lines).

though, and decided that as long as we could find enough cockles to fulfil it, would stick it out for at least that season. Then we too had to call it a day and we came home. We had made some good friends among the porters and staff at Hest Bank station; they let us use their cabin to eat our food, and to sleep in when we had to be up very early in the morning, though I remember I didn't get much sleep as the express trains to Scotland and the north rushed alongside the cabin.

The following year, I left school at the age of fourteen, and had to get accustomed to working with a horse and cart on my own. The horse was still very popular at that time, and, as well as for fishing, was used regularly for delivering goods in the towns and villages. The farmers used them too, as the tractor was not known around here then.

Farm horses of course were too heavy and too slow for our job out on the sands. What we wanted was the vanner type: the kind which could trot when asked, or when we were being chased by the tide. Many such horses were brought over from Ireland and bought by the cabbies for work on the promenade. Their season was the summer and the horses were worked very hard. We knew most of the cabbies and Dad had an eye for a good horse, so when we were wanting another one we went over to Morecambe to watch the horses at work. We would pick out a likely one and ask the owner if he would be selling after the season was over. Sometimes he would rather sell than keep the animal through the winter, eating his head off. We would often get the chance of riding on the cab, to see how the horse performed among traffic. If we thought he would be suitable for our work, Dad would ask for a week's trial, if possible, before buying. Usually the owner would be agreeable. We found most of the horses we bought were good for the job, but we wanted a trial to see if the animal would take to the water. What he would be doing from then on was something very different from trotting up and down the promenade in the summer weather.

Shrimping, another important source of our income, was done with a net trawled from the back of the cart, so our horses needed to be able to get on and move quickly at both the walk and the trot. The carts they had to pull were on tall wheels, so that we could go into fairly deep water without the catch of shrimps floating about in the cart bottom. The shrimp net was attached to a wooden beam 13ft 6in long, with strips of iron at the top to keep it from floating up. The wooden beam was dragged along the sand, levelling out the ridges and disturbing the shrimps, which then jumped over the beam to be carried into the net by the force of the water.

We always timed our arrival at the fishing grounds so that the tide in the river channels and other stretches of water used for trawling would still be on the ebb. We trawled downstream, so that the strong current helped the horse; we could not ask him to drag against the current. Even if we had done so, the slightest force of water would have caused the small-meshed shrimp net to lift from the bottom, and then the horse would be pulling a dead weight. The only time we could travel upstream was on the turn of the tide: we would usually make one trawl, then, as the tide built up and gathered speed, it was safest to haul in the nets and make for home.

There was a great deal to learn about shrimping with a horse and cart. With your horse going steady, you could judge what sort of a catch you had by taking hold of the rope and pulling the net towards you. When the time came for hauling it in, you would stop the horse, coil in the rope, lift the net on to the back of the cart, and then ask the horse to move on and turn upstream. This ran the tail of the net right back and clear of the cart. Had we not turned, the run of the water would have carried the tail-end of the net right under the cart and it would have got caught on the axle or wheel nuts. Then we would have been in real trouble. The horse got quite used to this turning, though when there was a row of horses and carts more or less in line with one another you needed to have an obedient animal. When the first horse started to turn, the next man had to get his net on to the back of the cart in quick time, otherwise it was almost impossible to pull in the net because of the current. If you were too slow and failed to get the net on, you had to turn the cart quickly downstream and try again.

Another thing I had to learn while shrimping was never to turn sharply with the net out where the movement of the water was swift, as the cart could quite easily be overturned. We always had a spare coil of rope in the cart in case the horse dropped out of his depth in the channel where we were shrimping. We could then let out some rope, to take the weight of the net off him and let him swim along more easily until his feet touched the bottom again. Then we would stop and pull in the spare rope. Such unforeseen things could be very frightening at the time. They have happened to me and, I think, to every other fisherman who has ever fished with a horse and cart. This particular danger usually occurs when a deep hole has been scoured by the tide, especially when the river is running close in to the shore and near to the rocks. It doesn't happen so often when you are clear of the channels and out into the bay itself.

Even so, there is danger if you are not wary, especially at certain times of the year, for example when there has been a very hot summer. The weather has a lot to do with how the tides alter the lie of the sand. In what we call 'old spots' — stretches of water which have little or no movement in them, you will sometimes find flow-holes have developed where the sand has formed into a series of waves, leaving water in the hollows, sometimes shallow, sometimes very deep. Some places are so bad that we have to keep well clear of them. Because the water is stirred up by the horse, it is impossible to judge their depth, and there is always the danger of the cart turning over. First one wheel goes down and then the other; it is only the buoyancy of the cart when it hits the water than can save the fisherman from disaster.

The shrimping season starts about March. It is never really any good earlier than this; if the winter has been hard, the water temperature is still very low, and March can be a month of all sorts of weather — hail, showers and cold winds. In winter, at the first sign of severe frost, the shrimps leave our fishing grounds, probably going to deeper, warmer waters. No one seems to know exactly where they go. If it were a question only of deeper waters, this would enable coastal trawlermen to continue with a longer season; but it seems that this is not so, and their whereabouts in winter is something of a mystery. Some people have suggested that they bury themselves deep in the sand in a kind of hibernation, to reappear in the spring when the water temperature rises.

The season is at its best from March to May, and from August until sometime towards the end of November, depending on the mildness of the weather. June and July, the warmest months, are no good for shrimping at all, as at this time jellyfish are found everywhere in the bay. These are small, round transparent nuisances, which we nickname the 'jujubes' because they look very much like little round sweets. They would all have to be picked out from the catch — a very tedious job — so we leave shrimping alone in those months of the year.

There are two other kinds of jellyfish found in the bay. The large non-stinging type looks very much like a chandelier. The other is a very nasty one of a silver-grey colour, with dark brown running through the centre. This, if touched, or even shaken out of the net, can sting very badly, with a sting much stonger than that of a nettle. Another stinger, but more effective still, is the weaver fish known to us Flookburgh fishermen as the 'Attapile'. It is six inches long, silver and brown in colour and when it is disturbed, poisoned barbs protrude from the top of its head. Fishermen usually get stung by these fish in the dark. When you have tipped your shrimps into the box, and are running your hand through them sorting out the seaweed and small flukes, suddenly you feel a terrible sharp pain which penetrates to the very bone, and you know what has happened. It is agony, and the only way to get relief from the pain is to urinate on the finger. This is an old-fashioned remedy but certainly works.

Whatever the difficulties, we were always optimistic, and worked hard to make a living. At the right time of the year, there were plenty of shrimps in both rivers, the Kent and the Leven, starting well up in the estuaries. Many a day it was quite usual to see a good number of horses pulling their carts, perhaps going under the subway at Grange-over-Sands station to start shrimping around the Holme Island area, or coming out from Pigeon Cote Lane, to the north of Humphrey Head, and then making their way up the sands towards the River Kent. They would all start trawling downriver, perhaps having three or four trawls. A good catch was three or four boxes full; the last trawl would be left in the tail-end of the net until we got home.

Around this time, 1947-48, there was still quite a lot of hand-netting for shrimps in the Kents Bank and Holme Island areas. This was done with a net attached to a beam much smaller than the ones we used. The fishermen had to wade into the channel and push the net before him. He could do this quite well, but the quality of the shrimps he caught was poor as he could not go into deep water. Small shrimps were plentiful in the shallow dykes, in those days, but even the hand-netter had to be wary or he would find himself going for a swim!

Finding a market for the shrimps was sometimes very difficult, and though for a while we had a good order from one of the northern coastal towns, we found later that we had a job to get the money. It was far too costly to have to make journeys to the other side of the bay just to chase the bad payers, so my sister and I decided to take a basket, lined with a white cloth, full of the really big shrimps we were getting at that time, and hawk them round the streets of Carnforth. We would set off, each with our basket, covered with white muslin, on the train. We both enjoyed going round the houses and meeting different people. They were good customers and once they knew the days we would be coming, they would leave a dish with their order and the money on the window sill. Carnforth was a very good fish town for us in those days. It seemed that as one market closed to us, another one opened. We felt luck was with us.

Then came a setback. Dad became ill so I had to take the horse and cart and go out to the cockling grounds. This was very soon after I had left school. My younger sister came along with me, and the other fishermen were very good and kept an eye on us while Dad was unable to work. My eldest sister had by this time gone as a probationer in a hospital, and made nursing her job from then on. We did fairly well; Mam managed to boil the cockles with our help, though we missed Dad terribly and had to keep asking him how to do this, that and the other. But this is the way to learn, and I could soon do the job quite well, young as I was.

Meanwhile we had found a spot where the shrimps were plentiful. But marketing them was becoming a problem, until Dad hit on the idea of salting them down in wooden barrels until such time as we could find a market. Salted hard, they could be kept indefinitely, and we could hold on to them until we could make money on them.

Such a time was just around the corner. In 1949, late one evening, a knock came on our door. On answering it we found a good-looking chap in his early fifties. He said he had been sent from London and would be interested in buying shrimps. He told us of the premises he had in mind, and said that until the firm got properly organised, he would collect all our shrimps from the door. This he did regularly, on an old butcher's bicycle! He carried the shrimps in a box on the front in the same way that the butcher's boy of old used to bring the meat round to the doors. The catches he collected from us were sent down to London, no doubt for the thriving markets there, where the hotels were beginning to use the lowly shrimp in some quantity. Later the collection of the shrimps was done in an old London taxi, which was a step up from the bicycle.

This was going to be a good thing for the village fishermen, and we ourselves were able to sell from the barrels the surplus shrimps we had stored. We were lucky to be the first to be called on by this man, as it was early days and he could only take shrimps from one or two fishermen until he got properly organised. Shrimping was to become our main job now that we had secured our orders, sold our surplus and had a market on our doorstep. There was no limit to what we could catch; we were limited only by the amount we could get 'picked'.

For the picking or shelling of the shrimps we were fortunate in having some very good workers. Theirs was the task of separating the husk from the fish. Before this could be done, however, the shrimps had to be properly boiled; this made all the difference to the work of the pickers, and Dad was an expert at the boiling process.

When shrimps are first caught they are a greyish colour, and almost transparent. They are emptied from the nets into boxes, and the crabs, small flukes and jellyfish are thrown back into the water. When the fisherman reaches home, the shrimps are put into a boiler — the old cast-iron type of washing boiler is still widely used in Flookburgh. The water must be right on the boil before putting them in, and then they are given a good stir round. This makes sure they are all evenly boiled. From the time of putting them in, they boil up for between ten and fifteen minutes for the first boiling. Less time is needed for the second and third boilings, as the water keeps its heat. They need to boil up three times and are stirred after each boiling. Then, after the third boiling, a few should be taken out into the open air. If they are ready, they will turn pink with a white speck showing which later disappears, leaving them a pinkish-brown colour. We then usually try to shell one or two to see if they are easy to pick.

In years gone by, when the shrimps were taken out of the boiler, they were spread on hessian sacks to drain and dry. Then they would be riddled and the small ones taken back to the sands where the seagulls would be waiting for them. Today, shrimps have to be riddled out on the sands alive, instead of bringing back the whole catch; the law requires that the small ones be put back into the water to grow on. Nor are hessian sacks used any longer; it is impossible to get them, now that they have been widely replaced by plastic, and today the shrimps are drained and dried in trays.

As well as our regular pickers we were able to get some extra helpers who were really good. These were mainly Polish and Italian families who were housed nearby, on what had been, during the war, an RAF training camp. The families were shown how to shell the shrimps, and after a week or so they got the hang of it; they were doing us a real favour and also making themselves some extra cash. For several years these people were allowed to stay in their huts — Nissen huts they were called. I suppose they were really glad to have them, after what they had been through during the war. They kept these homes spotlessly clean, and with their little gardens surrounding them, they looked very cosy. We found these families easy to get on with, and very quietly spoken. Some of them moved away to the towns where they could find better-paid work than was available in this area, but a few stayed on, to settle into the village life, and are still here to this day.

Having a ready market for our shrimps, we found more outsiders — builders, joiners, tradesmen of all kinds — leaving their jobs and starting up on the sands while the going was good. They all wanted a share in the good times, which was fair up to a point, but it made for a lot of jealousy amongst the regulars. Then, too, some of these outsiders never knew when they had taken enough. Sometimes twice a day to the sands they would go, and even at weekends. This was sure to make it bad for us regulars, who had no other way of making a living. Down went the price when the markets were glutted, and we were back to where we started. These people couldn't see it that way though. Another result was that large quantities of small shrimps were brought off the sands, only to be boiled, riddled and fed to the ducks, or even carted back to the sands where the gulls would eat them. This of course reduced the future catch. It was a great pity, but at the time no one realised what the long-term effect would be. Meanwhile, on our way to the shrimping grounds we had to travel over the areas where we had cockled the previous winter, and found a very good show of 'wheaat', as we call the very young cockles, which, by the end of the next shrimping season, would be big enough to be gathered.

Shrimping was not only done in the daytime. About the end of August, we often started working at night. Usually, in the areas where we were working, when the tides were very low and the weather calm, conditions would be ideal. Low tides meant that shrimps came into the shallow water and gathered near the side of the channel; if you could find a good place, the shallower the water, the thicker the shrimps would be. You could even get out of the carts while the horse just plodded on steadily, with the net out, and you could see, by the light of the torch we always carried, the shrimps jumping over the beam into the net. It really was a sight to see!

Each night there used to be a rush for the side of the channel where most of the shrimps would be. No one wanted to be the inside cart, at night, working where the water was deep and the shrimps sparse. Sometimes it would be fairly level ground we were working on and our chances of a good catch were evened out. On the other hand, perhaps a mile or so along the channel the banking would drop straight down and the water would be deep, levelling off towards the other side. Then the outside cart would do well, with its net half in the water and half on the sand, while the inside carts in the deep water found only a few shrimps, and the rest of their catch would be crabs and suchlike. This was just the opposite of the catches in daylight hours, when the shrimps would go into the deeper water.

Soon after I got my own horse and cart, when I was in my early teens, I went out shrimping with Dad and a few other fishermen in the late evening. In those days, we used to keep to fairly shallow places, never more than cart-bottom deep, though some of the dykes would be a hundred or two hundred yards wide. In these dykes shrimps used to lie all the time. West Dyke, Shell Dyke, Stocky and Cod 'oller were very good spots just then. We never dreamt of going into deep water in those days, but now the bay has silted up and the shrimps have gone with the water. It is the same with the codlings: Cod 'oller was full of good cod at that time, when the water was deep.

It was a calm night when we set off, but there was no moon, and no wind at all. We started to move into the channel, and as the horses hoofs hit the water, the splashes were all lit up just like fireworks being let off — like sparklers. The horse I had that night was fairly new to the job and had never before seen the foxfire, as we called this phosphorescent glowing on the water, and he was petrified. Every movement of the horse's hoofs in the water sent up a shower of sparkling drops into the dark night. As the cart in front of me moved up into the channel, its wheels threw a cascade of shining water right in my horse's path and frightened him so much that I couldn't control him. He would keep making one way. I pulled on the reins but he took no notice and I thought I would get drowned, as he was going in a fair way to turn the cart over. He just wanted to get anywhere out of the foxfire. In the end, Dad had to take my horse and I took his more experienced animal.

The foxfire has to be seen to be believed. When you have tipped your shrimps into the box and you are running your hand through them, you don't need a torch; they are all aglow. The sparks flicker round the spokes of the wheels, the hubs, the nets. You can see the mesh and the whole shape of the nets all glowing with phosphorescence. If only we could have photographed it! But you can never tell when it will occur. I have seen it only a very few times in my life, in spite of all my experience on the sands. Shrimping with a horse and cart, however, by activating the water, shows to the full the true brilliance of the foxfire.

3 Fishing with Horse and Cart

Horses are like people; there are no two alike. Some you can trust with your life, and we often have to do just that. They can have quite different temperaments, some nervous, some bold and others very placid. In a tight corner, a quiet horse would bring you out safely; but with a young frisky horse, unused to work on the sands and in the water, you could easily find yourself with a tragedy on your hands.

Such a thing happened when two young lads decided to go out into the bay for a couple of bags of cockles after the late tide. They set off in fine style, with their cart and a very spirited young horse, just as it was coming dusk. Off through the village they went and down to the shore. The horse was a real high stepper. 'Too much blood in it,' was Dad's opinion. 'A bit of a cross is what you need for work out there on the sands.'

Away they went over the rocky foreshore, out into the bay and on towards the cockle beds. But they never picked a single cockle that night. As soon as their horse felt his feet going down into a few inches of mud, he wouldn't heed at all. They tried to rein him in but he just didn't answer. On he went and by now the night had closed in. Where they were they didn't know. Suddenly, the horse went over a banking and down into more muddy sand. This scared him afresh and he was now galloping, completely out of control. All their gear — cockle baskets, boxes, sacks, everything — was flying in all directions. Luckily the cart stayed on its wheels, though they were covering the ground at breakneck speed. They had lost all sense of time, only trying to hold on to the cart at all costs. Any hope of stopping the runaway had long since gone, but now, as they splashed through a shallow dyke, they felt they were getting on to higher ground. All at once, they felt a wind blowing and then, above the noise of the frightened animal and the creaking cart, they heard a roaring like the sound of an express train — the tide.

It comes up the rivers and dykes which flow through Morecambe Bay faster than anyone can run: the bay can be completely flooded in less than half an hour. Their only hope was to leave the horse and cart and try to find their way to the shore. The tide had almost reached the wheels of the cart, with the horse still going hell for leather. In no time at all, the cart was lifting on the water and was soon floating; the horse was now up to his belly and had to start swimming. That was the last the lads saw of him, or so they thought. Listening for any sound which would give them some idea of how far they were from the shore, they heard the clock at Grange-over-Sands strike ten. They felt as if they had been careering round the bay for hours! A beam from the headlamps of a car shone up in the dark sky. With relief they made for the shore and found themselves just beyond the Carter Road railway crossing; soaking wet with mud and water, they set off on the long walk back to Flookburgh.

Early next morning, the two of them made their way along the shore to see whether there were any signs of the horse or the cart having been washed up by the tide. A few pieces of splintered wood scattered on the rocks was all they found. They set off towards the promenade and, to their amazement, there on the rocks stood the horse! The remains of the broken shafts were still hanging from the harness, but he seemed little worse for his ordeal. There was a graze or two on his flanks, but no other damage. Whether he had kicked the cart to pieces in his frenzied struggle to survive, or whether the cart had come to grief on the rocks and so given him his chance, no one could say.

As well as the speed of the tide, there are other perils of the bay. I have been out there at low tide, in a gale, when it was exactly like a sandstorm. You could not see anything, apart from the sand, and it was a peculiar sensation, with sand stinging your face and hands, and getting in your eyes. The horses were terrified by this wall of sand coming at them. The only thing to do in weather like this is to turn your back to it; so we turned our carts, giving the horses what cover we could. Most frightening of all for the horses was the way the very ground seemed to be blowing away from under them. Luckily, such sandstorms are not very common. They only occur when the tide has been low for a few days, leaving a large area of dry sand, and when the winds are fierce. I have not noticed the sand blowing so much when using a tractor, maybe because you are higher up than with a cart.

One thing a tractor cannot do is to follow the tracks you have made on the outward journey, as a good horse would. A horse new to the sands would take a little time to get used to following the tracks, but an experienced animal was able to follow them, even in the dark. You could even sit with your back to the horse and he would bring you home. But once the tide started to rise up, it took the wheel marks out of the sand and you would have to drive. If it was a fine night and a westerly wind, there were always lights showing. We could see the lights of Morecambe, or, if we looked to the west, there were the Barrow lights and Peel lighthouse flashing away; over to the eastern side of the bay, there was the light on Jenny Brown's Point. All these lights we used as markers when out on the sands at night.

Another thing which determined our area of fishing was the wind. If it was blowing a strong westerly, we would go to the west; with an easterly wind, we went to the east. There was a good reason for this. You see, in Morecambe Bay there are many different kinds of seaweed which come up with the tide. This seaweed, muck as we call it, is always sucked into the wind; the wind doesn't blow it away. Therefore, if it was blowing out of the west we went over to the west to put our nets in, and the muck would be on the other side from where we were working. If it was blowing out of the west and you went to the east, you would find the spot where you wanted to shrimp, drop your nets, and they would be loaded with muck before you had gone a hundred yards. In order to fish safely and successfully, all this had to be learnt: I was lucky in having the experience of my Father to call on.

He also taught me, for example, never to go through large sheets of shallow water. This can be as dangerous as putting your head in a noose, especially in fog. When you go out there, you want to come back, so you must keep to the dry places, and I am always careful to notice everything as I go along. To one who follows the sands, everything has a meaning. In particular, you have to keep a sharp eye open all the time for any change in the way the tide has left the sand and the dykes. All the dykes have names, given to them by the fishermen over the years. You are not, of course, going over the same area every day; since the sands change with every tide, you need some landmarks, and the smaller drains or dykes don't change quite so much as the main river channels. Even the ridges on the sand can tell much to one who has been brought up to notice every little difference, as I was.

People may wonder why we never used a compass. We were not brought up to use one. We did try them for a time, while fishing with carts, but without much success. They may be all right for boats, but in our particular conditions we often found ourselves doubting the compass, which did not help at all!

It is, of course, only too easy to find yourself in danger. When I was a youngster, I was coming out one day between Pigeon Cote Lane and Humphrey Head. The channel was running round, right down the shore, past Kents Bank, close in to the rocks, about a quarter of a mile from Humphrey Head. We had crossed with the horses and trawled up, then turned and trawled down on the inside of the channel. We couldn't go in too near to the rocks as there were places where it was too deep and the horses would have been out of their depth. Mine was the middle horse and cart, and all of a sudden, my horse went into his collar to pull hard, and jerked as if it was too difficult. The fore-end of the cart creaked; I slipped my rope, thinking I had got fast to something. The horse tried again to pull hard on his collar and gave a jerk which made the cart shudder. I knew then that I really was fast.

It was the first time I had experienced this sort of thing, so I was rather frightened. I let the horse take the strain again, and the same thing happened: he couldn't move the cart at all. I had a very strong horse, and he really tried, but the net was completely stuck. I released more rope, until I had released the lot. The water would be about cart-bottom deep; I remember looking as I let the rope out, and seeing it wavering on top of the water. I stopped the horse pulling, and turned him round, while one of the other fishermen put his net up on the back of his cart and came back to me. I had no idea what to do, but we both jumped out of our carts, up to our bellies in the water, and scraped away to try to find out what was holding the net. The wooden beam was broken, and the iron bar, which should keep the net from floating, was bent double. The beam had been caught fair and square in the middle, and snapped in two.

We got the net free, after a great deal of struggling, and found that the cause of all the trouble was an old iron bar, like a corkscrew, which could have been put in years before, perhaps right out in the bay, as a marker. It had got washed in towards the shore and left upright in the sand by the tide. It caused me a great deal of trouble. I had to go home, my day's fishing lost. The blacksmith straightened out the iron bar, and I also had to visit the joiner for a new beam, then go home and fit up the net again. It is a full day's work fitting up a beam and bar on a shrimp net, so it was altogether a very expensive day for me. We had to keep our eyes open in that area after that. We marked the spot by the rocks nearby, noticing just where it had happened, and in future we kept out of that place.

There were days when you had trouble with the horse too. One day a horse 'took stek', that is he stopped on account of nerves. We were in very deep water and it was almost flood tide, and there seemed nothing we could do. The fisherman even went alongside the horse and tried to coax him, with another horse by his side, but he wouldn't move. The lad got out into my cart, and we were about to leave both horse and cart when we decided to have one more try. We loosened the cart, so the horse was free, and some of the men 'brayed' him, that is beat him, and eventually they pulled him out. They couldn't do anything about the cart, which got moved by the tide and buried out in the bay. Years afterwards, it was washed up and the men hauled it out, but it was by then as heavy as three or four carts. Its condition was just as good as on the day it went in, because, you see, the salt water had pickled it.

Many accidents did happen. Horses got stuck in the quicksands, carts were overturned crossing the rivers. A horse might refuse to budge or sometimes would give in altogether.

I well remember the first time I saw a horse getting stuck in the quicksands. We had been shrimping over the west side of the bay, in the Ulverston channel, near the River Leven opposite Baycliffe and Bardsea villages, and had a good catch of shrimps.

We were making our way home, just pulling our nets round, when suddenly we saw what was happening. Some of the fishermen had come out of the river much higher up than us, in a really bad place. We heard them shouting, and we looked up and saw horses being asked to do the near-impossible. . .

The first horses over manage to make the side. The fishermen take no heed of the quivering sand. The quicksand quivers as if it is angry, and about to burst open and swallow up anyone or anything that dares to tread upon it. The horses do their utmost to obey the bawling of the young men. 'Spread out', we shout. 'Split yer tracks. . . Goo on, make new ground,' are our cries. 'Keep 'em going.' But all our shouting has no effect on the last horse to cross. The sand gives way, opens up like nothing on this earth, and down goes the horse in a horrible struggle, using all his energy to the last, but to no avail. Then, all at once, there is silence. The only sound is the heavy breathing of the animal engulfed in the sand.

Then comes a sudden change. Where the horse has gone down and where the others had trodden, the sand settles hard and firm. The horse is in about halfway up his belly and the cart is also mired. The tide is due very shortly, as it was on the turn when we came out from shrimping. What can be done? As quickly as possible, a volunteer holds the other horses, as they seem to sense there is trouble and we don't want them taking fright. All the other fishermen help at what seems an impossible task. One lad finds a spade; another tries to loosen the harness, but it is well under the sand and can't be cut through. In the little time that is left, the shafts of the cart are hacked through with the spade, but although the horse is now free of the cart, he is well and truly held solid in the sand. We don't give in. We dig the sand away, but as fast as we dig it justs fills in again. 'Now, that's it,' someone says. 'There's nowt more we can do.'

'TIDE!' shouts another. The bore is fast coming up the river.

Saddened by all this, we all make out on to the bank for safety, watching helplessly as the wave of the oncoming tide passes the horse and slowly creeps up, about to cover him. He disappears under the swirling tide. Every man has his own thoughts as we stand there, watching silently. . . Suddenly there is an almighty splashing and the horse emerges from the frothy, turbulent water and starts to swim towards the side, with us urging him on. A couple of the chaps wade in and catch hold of the reins, bringing him to the side of the channel. We calm him down as best we can and walk him home, where we help the young fellow to give him a good rubbing down. We see him bedded down on a thick heap of straw, and Dad and I go home for the night.

Next morning we went off to see how the horse had fared after the ordeal of the day before, and found him seemingly none the worse. We had decided it would be best not to give him anything to eat the night before, just a drink of water, as he was very upset, but now he was calmly eating some good clover hay. The lads took him out on the sands cockling a few more times, to see how he would react to the water, but they found he would not go into the dykes at all. It was evident that he would never get over such an experience, so the only thing to do was to find him a good home on a farm, where he could work on dry land. Dad knew of a farmer who was only too glad to have a reliable horse, so Rob, as he was called, found a tranquil life where he would never again have to face the perils of the sands of Morecambe Bay.

I remember doing a bit of horse trading out on the sand. This was just before I went into the army at eighteen to do two years' national service, which was compulsory at that time. I had been watching this horse for some time and had seen how quickly he got over the ground. Dad said he wouldn't do for shrimping, but, being young, I wanted to have something that would leave the other horses standing. Speed was what I wanted — none of your plodding quiet horses for me!

So I went out on to the sand to meet the fisherman who was from over the other side of the bay. We had no telephone in those days, but of course you got to know people, fishing together out in the bay. I already had a good horse, a handsome animal but he was a bit too slow for my liking. So we did a trade there on the sand — I took his horse and he took mine. I came back across the River Kent, on towards Guide's Farm; off we went up the hill and along the top road and through Allithwaite village. I was hoping everyone would see what a lively young horse I'd got. We passed motor cars and farm carts; we passed everything on the road. He really could move — he could fly! Then, when I got him home, Dad came out and took one look at it. 'He'll be no good to thee, lad,' he said. 'For t'Derby mebby, but not for shrimpin', I can tell thee. T'orse yer swopped fer that were worth ten o' 'im. He's not worth a taatie.'

I took him out the next day and we started shrimping. I hardly had time to get the net out before he was off. When I asked him to turn he was so quick that the cart nearly turned over. After two trawls, I decided to call it a day. I had a couple of boxes of shrimps and I barely had time to get the net, with the last catch in it, on to the cart. When I came out of the water with the net across the back of the cart, that horse just couldn't wait. He set off full ding — trot, not gallop, full trot — and when we got to some rough sand, the net would bounce, bounce, bounce. The shrimps were flying all ways; I had no time to sort them as I would have been able to do with a quiet horse. It was all I could do to hold him to the road.

I kept him until I went into the army. Then another fisherman took him, thinking he could tame him but he never made anything of him either, and soon sold him again. This time, he went to a cabbie in Morecambe and I saw him trotting gaily along the promenade, pulling an old-fashioned landau full of happy holidaymakers; the faster he went, the more they laughed and shrieked. He was in his element at last.

I was very glad of his speed, though, one day when I went out to get a few cockles. It was a misty morning, and I was keeping a weather eye open for anything unusual out there on the sands, when I noticed a couple of chaps digging bait, much farther out than I thought they ought to be. But it was a few hours to tide time, so I went on with my work. I had staked the horse and given him a bit of hay to keep him quiet. I soon got all the cockles I needed, so I yoked up Flash, then loaded the cockles on to the cart and was ready for off, when I looked towards the place where I had seen the two fellows digging. I thought they would have gone long since, but with my good eyesight I could see one chap waving his arms about. We soon got near enough for me to see there was trouble: one of the chaps had gone down in the quicksands. Speed was what we needed, and with Flash, speed was what we had. I thought of my Dad's words — 'He'll be nah good to thee' — as we careered over the sand. That morning we needed just such a horse.

When I got near enough to see clearly how things were, I got a coil of rope which I always carried in the cart. You never knew when you might need rope, shovel, axe or whatever, out there. I made a noose on the end of the rope and threw it to the man, who by this time was almost waist deep in the mire. With some encouragement from his mate, who was nearly frantic, he managed to catch the rope. I had never done much lassoing, but it went over his head, and I shouted, 'Git this under yer armpits, git yer arms through it and pull it tight. 'Old on now.' Flash, as game as ever, pulled on his collar, and slowly, out the man came. It was easier than I had thought; I just wondered why the chap had gone so red in the face, when I thought he would have been white with fright. He came out stark naked! The suction was so strong that it had pulled his trousers right off. We had to wrap him in the horse blanket and we took him home on my cart. He had had such a bad scaring that I was sure he wouldn't be out on Morecambe Bay for a good long time.

Looking on the bright side, his mate said, 'Good job it didn't 'appen near the prom, or you would 'ave 'ad a row of 'olidaymakers getting an eyeful!' Then he added, 'It could'a bin worse. It might 'ave 'appened on a Friday, and yer week's wages would'a bin down there, with yer trousers.'

Towards the end of the time when we used horses for shrimping, I got a damn good horse from Barrow, where one of the big firms was going over to motor vehicles. This horse was a strapping strawberry roan, seventeen hands two high. With Dad following Barrow market, we had already seen the horse, which used to pull a big milk lorry every morning. He was a fine-looking animal, and would have made a good hunting horse. I never dreamt that one day I should own him, but when the firm came to sell, a farmer near Barrow put in a tender for the horses and he got four. Dad went to see the farmer, who let us have this one at a reasonable price, making himself perhaps a bit of a profit, and we brought him back. We had a small piece of land on the coast road at that time. We yoked the horse up and went out on the Bardsea beach, just as the tide was coming in; he went into the water just as if he had been doing it all his life. It was good flat sand there, and he did well. I was really chuffed with him. I shrimped with him once or twice and kept him all through the winter, when we were doing very little, just a bit of cockling, which was nothing for a big, leggy horse like this.

Spring came, a cold spring; as soon as I had him out shrimping, how that horse bossed me about! Where he had been so good the previous year, in any weather, he was now almost unmanageable. Because I had the biggest horse, mine was the inside cart as we struck into the channel. It was a fairly wild day, blowing and blustery, with surf coming up against us. The horse reared as each wave hit us. Up and down he went. What a scare was on then! The others were for pushing me into the deep water at first, but when they saw the horse rearing, with his front legs lashing out, they were all for trying to get out of the way, thinking something was going to happen. When we got to the side, somebody shouted, 'Put a bag o're it 'ead.' I hadn't a bag, so I took off my jacket and fastened that over his head; then I went to the outside position, but the horse wasn't having it. He kept running back on the net. I gave up after that, because the beggar could have drowned me; being such a big horse, he tipped the cart right up, and it was like trying to hold on to the side of a wall! I went off that horse from then on, because when you are going into such deep water you need a good steady animal, something reliable. He too went to Morecambe promenade, where he would be doing a job similar to his previous one in Barrow, pulling the milk float.

We always found that a cross-bred horse, one with a bit of 'feathering' about it, was better for our work. Feathering is the term used to describe the growth of long, fine hair on the horse's legs; it is only found to any extent on the heavier type of horse. On the hind legs, the hair usually starts just below the hocks and around the fetlock joints, and hanging down over the heels; on the forelegs it starts just behind and below the knee joint and continues down to the fetlock in the same way. The finer-boned, more spirited horses are clean-legged, lacking this hair. As Dad used to say, 'If they 'ave a bit o' blood in 'em, keep off 'em. They're no good to us; too fiery.'

A very sad occasion was when we had to watch a young

horse drown. He was a highly strung animal that thought of nothing but going ahead. We were shrimping much lower down on the sands that day than we normally did, over the west side of the bay in the Leven channel. Away above us, was a bar — a fording place which could be crossed quite comfortably at a certain after the tide was on the ebb. The older fishermen and we youngsters usually stuck together, and we had decided to trawl down the near side of the river, as the shrimps were plentiful. Two of the other fishermen had other ideas. Possibly thinking there were enough of us working this side of the river, they crossed to the other side where the water was about cart-bottom deep, and trawled down the opposite side from us. The water was very wide and the river was deep in the middle, way out of a horse's depth.

On hauling our nets, we found we had really good catches, far better than on previous occasions. Seeing how well we had done, the other two hauled their nets and found them almost empty. This upset them and they started to cross to our side. The safest way would have been for them to go back up their side of the river and across where they had crossed before, but they were in too much of a hurry and tried to make it straight through to us. The horses were soon off their feet and swimming. A horse can swim with the cart, so long as the net is not dragging behind; but it takes ages to turn a horse once he is off his feet, and there was a fairly strong current running where we were shrimping. One of the men had a sensible, steady horse; this quiet animal was able to turn, and eventually touch his feet on the bottom and made the journey back up the far side and through the ford to us. But the excitable, young horse following behind, had only one thing in his mind. As soon as he got off his feet, he started lunging up in the air. The lad couldn't get him to turn and go back, so the only thing to do was to try to come straight across to us; but it was not to be. The depth of water the horse found himself in scared him and he reared up. The net was washed off the cart, and the rope got entangled round the fisherman's legs, pulling him into the river. After much struggling, he managed to free himself of his thigh boots and oilskins and swim to the nearest cart. The net was now like an anchor and the horse could do no more than swim round in circles. Two of the men attempted to reach the horse to try to cut the harness, but the force of the incoming tide swirled them up-channel, and they had to be hauled out with ropes which the others threw to them. It was hopeless. Nothing could be done to save the horse now: no one could have got near to him because of his lashing forelegs. The poor creature tired as the tide rushed over him and eventually drowned. Horse and cart were washed up on the shore a few days later, the nets having been torn to shreds, at last releasing the cart and the dead animal.

The death of my own horse was another upsetting event. It happened one night when I was out with a couple of other fishermen. I had what I thought was a grand horse — a good mover, and steady when pulling the net. I hadn't had him many weeks when this happened. We reached the shrimping grounds just as the moon was coming up. It was a lovely summer night, perfect for shrimps. We came across some flow-holes, which, as I mentioned earlier, are common at this time of the year. We were just about to trawl and had dropped our nets off and splashed into the night, in water about a foot deep, when there was a sudden drop to three feet or so and my horse fell. I naturally thought he had stumbled, as he was fairly new to the job, but he lay there and didn't even struggle. I jumped off the cart at once, grabbed his head and held it above water. The other two fishermen, seeing what had happened, couldn't get their nets on quickly enough, and drove to the side where one man stayed with their horses while the other waded in to help me. I knew by now that my horse had not just stumbled. His nostrils were wide, his eyes staring and his breathing heavy and irregular. Going down as he had, the harness had tightened, so nothing could be loosened. I always carried a knife, so I cut the top strap from the hames, and also the leather back band and breaching straps. Now he was free of the cart. We thought he would get up but he didn't. We used all our strength and energy in pulling, and eventually had to use force. He came up unsteadily on to his legs and we led him to the side. We found that, because of his weight on the shafts as he lay in the water, they had been partly submerged in the sand, so the only way to get the cart out was to go in with one of the other horses and tow it out. This worked, and towards the side we came. As the harness was cut, we decided to tow my cart behind one of the others, while I led my horse slowly home.

I bedded him down in his stable and rang the veterinary surgeon. He was a very good man and came at once. After a thorough examinaion, he told me the horse had suffered a severe heart attack. He gave him an injection and said we would see how he was in the morning, but he didn't give much hope; and early next morning as I opened the stable door, I could see the horse lying dead. It was a great blow, as I had just got attached to him and he was so steady and reliable at the job.

We had another horse to look for now and as always, a great deal would depend upon our choice. When you get into difficulties, a good, placid, steady horse would bring you out of anywhere. You could stake your life on it. In fact, that was what we were doing most of the time, out there on the sands.

4 The Changing Scene

As time moved on, 'progress' came to Flookburgh. It would have been around 1954 that one of the fishermen decided that he could no longer get enough with his old horse and cart — he wanted to be different. A tractor on the sands! Never been heard of before! Rumours were flying round the village: 'So and so 'as got 'issel' a DAMN BIG TRACTOR. Serve 'issel' reet if 'e gits stuck out theer, 'e'll git mar than 'e's bargained for.'

Of course, one set another off, and before long, everybody had a tractor. They were petrol Fergusons, but in those days they were not fitted with good splash guards over the wheels as they are today. Everything and everybody got sand and water everywhere. When we got home, there was a pile of sand to be cleared off the trailer, from the splashing of the water as we came through the dykes and gulleys at speeds we could never have made with a horse and cart. We were always trying to beat the others in getting home first. It was a novelty, driving a tractor, and there was no speed limit out there on the sands.

But the progress was short lived. The cockling grounds were not to last us so long now, as the families with a tractor and trailer could bring home three times the weight of cockles they could carry on the horse-drawn carts. Also, several members of the family could go to help gather the cockles, making the job much easier. A couple of winters' cockling and the beds were thinning out rapidly.

Eventually the cockles became so sparse that it was not economical to run the tractors, so they were laid up. Sand and salt water played havoc with them; I remember Dad and I gave ours a good clean down and a greasing, and a touch up with a coat of paint. We found, after a while, that a tractor company was buying up tractors from people in the village, and changing the engines over from petrol to TVO — tractor vaporising oil, or paraffin, with later modifications to diesel, before re-selling them.

S.P.M.B.—D

It was grand after the tractors had ceased tearing about on the sands. Now, back to our horses and carts — to something reliable and something which would not rust with the salt water, or maybe not start when cold. This could be a frightening experience, especially when the tide was coming in. For the next few years, cockling was only done in a very small way and mainly for the local markets. We went out once or twice a week prior to market days.

Most of the fishing families had a market garden or a smallholding as a sideline for when there was a lull in fishing. Some of them had a greenhouse and were thus able to grow early crops for the markets at Barrow-in-Furness and Kendal. Our own market garden was doing well and we needed some help with the weeding, so I looked around at the youngsters in the village. One lad called Bill, who was the son of one of the men I had known when I was in the Flookburgh band, a few years before, seemed the sort of lad we wanted; as his father had died quite recently, his mother was only too glad for the boy to earn a bit of spare cash. So Bill came after school and at weekends to help us in the garden, and a good help he was too. He would turn his hand to anything, helping Dad to load the van ready for market, weeding and transplanting. We always grew a big bed of outdoor lettuce which we tried to get ready early to sell at the best price in the market. We also had two good greenhouses, 60ft by 16ft. In these we were able to grow very early crops for the Easter market, providing we trenched in a load of good old farmyard manure. When the first crops were cleared, we followed them with tomatoes and quite a lot of bedding plants, though we had to have a little heat to start these off.

As well as this, I was following the sands full-time with the horse and cart, for both cockles and shrimps for the market. Bill was such a steady, dependable lad that I asked him if he would like to come out on the sands with me. He jumped at the idea and soon got used to handling the horse and cart, taking to the work as if he had been born to it. I was glad to let him drive, as I would much rather walk than ride over the sands to the cockle beds across the bay.

Bill always wore a pair of knee boots with leggings pulled up over them, but he would never put the leggings on until we were well out on the sands. One day I was walking ahead as usual, when, glancing round, as I did from time to time, I saw him flying through the air over the back of the cart. The horse was racing towards me and stopped when it reached me. I ran back to Bill, who had already picked himself up, fortunately none the worse for his tumble. He had evidently been pulling the leggings up over his rubber boots while standing up in the cart. The peculiar noise of rubber on rubber must have startled the horse, and he went off at the gallop, with what might have been disastrous results. However, Bill was young and able to take this sort of thing without much hurt. We were passing a dyke just as it happened, so we christened it 'Legging Dyke' after that.

Bill was in his element when we started shrimping, and I let him drive the cart through gullies and dykes, where the water was almost up to the floor of the cart. Back home, we would boil our catch, which Dad would take to Barrow market where it was soon sold.

Eventually Bill persuaded me to buy an old tractor. It was a David Brown Cropmaster TVO, and it certainly was old, having a starting handle to go with it. It would only start after a bit of coaxing. We never had any trouble getting the horse to start on a cold morning; just a touch on the reins and we would be on our way. The tractor was a different matter altogether, and there was cursing and swearing going on until at last the engine came to life. There was a small tank of petrol for starting, then as the engine warmed up you turned over from petrol to paraffin TVO. It used to splutter like hell if you turned over too soon. Petrol was so much dearer than paraffin that of course, being novices at this procedure, we tried to save the petrol, thinking that when we were out on the sands we might run out of it miles from anywhere. Later we got more used to the tractor's ways and learnt to trust it, venturing farther and farther away from the safety of the shore. We only used the tractor for cockling and it certainly got us over the bay much quicker than the horse and cart. We didn't pull a trailer at this time, but a platform was built out at the back of the tractor to carry a couple of hundredweight or so and all the gear we needed.

We were often out before daylight and it was a grand feeling coming home up over the marsh, with the sun just rising and the smell of the summer hay waftng over from the distant fields. . .

We hear the bellowing of the cows as the early-rising farmer takes his herd in for milking. A startled hare stops as we rattle by; he sits up, looks around and sees that we are not interested in him, then takes off at his bounding pace for the far pastures. As we come on to the road which leads to the village, the only noise is the rumbling of our old tractor. Coming through the village, the billowing smoke from the cottage chimneys shows that people are rising, ready to start the daily routine. We put the tractor away, unload the cockles, and feel a glow of satisfaction that we have done so well, so early in the morning, before most people have even thought of getting out of their beds. . .

I had done no more than pass the time of day with Bill's mother up to this time, though I knew something of the family from Bill. One evening when we had been out after a late tide, I took Bill back home, and he asked his mother whether I could come in for a cup of tea. This was the beginning of a lasting relationship. Bill's mother, Olive Nickson, had four children. Bill was the eldest, then came Robert, a quiet lad. Diane was a very pretty little girl, the image of her mother, and Paul, the baby, was just over a year old. I have always been able to get on well with children and these four seemed happy to have me around, but my visits, like the rest of my life, were governed by the tides. This meant that sometimes I didn't see Olive for several days.

Out on the sands, going across the miles, I thought about the future and wondered whether it was too soon to ask Olive if she had ever thought of marrying again. I decided not to be in too much of a hurry, and so my visits went on as usual, just taking Bill home, and perhaps staying for a bit of supper and watching television for half an hour or so. I would often have baby Paul on my knee while his mother got some supper ready for us all, and little Diane would sit by my chair chattering away as children do. The pattern of my days was changing; I spent as much time as work would let me with Olive and her family, and we came to know each other very well.

I had to work out in my mind, what I would have to do. Until now I had worked for my father and never had a wage. So far I had not felt the need of much money. Dad gave me whatever I wanted for all necessities and I hadn't bothered about anything further than that. Now, all this would have to be thought out. If I married, I would have to have a weekly wage or go out for myself. I decided I would ask Olive the very next time I went along to see her. We had known each other now for near on two years and I felt that all the family accepted me, so I was fairly sure what her answer would be. She thought that we should wait a while longer to make absolutely certain of our feelings for each other, so it was not until 30 October 1961 that we had our quiet wedding at St John's church in Flookburgh.

We lived at the house where Olive had lived with her family for the next two years, and during this time young Bill continued to come out on to the sands with me. On 3 January 1963 our daughter Jean was born, which added to our happiness.

The next set of cockles, meanwhile, had been found over on the other side of Morecambe Bay, between Silverdale and Bolton-le-Sands. Years had gone by since the large area of cockles at Hest Bank had brought together the fishing families just after the war. In 1960 this happened again, but by then Dad had bought his land and greenhouse, with a small business on Barrow market, where he had a stall. I went out cockling with Bill, and we boiled our catch to be sold on the stall, along with whatever produce we got from the land. Going to the market on only three days a week, Dad had plenty of time to look after the market garden and greenhouse, providing plenty of fresh vegetables for ourselves and for the market.

One advantage now was that most of the fishermen had acquired some kind of transport of their own. Most of them used vans to travel round to Silverdale instead of the railway, which was not always so easy to fit in with the tides. Also, everyone was back using tractors again. This meant, of course, that fuel had to be taken round the bay almost every day.

The first winter out in the new grounds was terribly cold. Snow and ice for weeks on end made the journey round a dangerous one. The narrow roads and sudden corners nearly had us in the ditch many a time, but eventually we got used to all the hazards. The farmers looked after our tractors, just as they had looked after our horses and carts in earlier years, though some of the men would leave theirs on the marsh. This meant that after a really cold night the tractors refused to start, and we had to lend a hand, towing them down the marsh to get them going at almost every tide. Conditions were often very severe, as it is always very much colder over on the Morecambe side of the bay.

What a racket those old tractors made! Some of them had no exhaust system, just a straight length of old pipe. On the mornings when the tide went out early, the villagers didn't need an alarm clock. The noise was enough to wake the dead. But we heard no grumbles — the new sounds had become part of the daily routine of the village.

There was only one route out on to the sands. In time, the track across this very long stretch of marsh became worn so deep that it was getting dangerous to use — in fact almost impossible. Trailer wheels were cutting in so deeply, as they carted their heavy load of cockles from the shore, that the tractors were almost dragging on their bellies. Some of the men tried making a new track a short distance from the old one, but as often as not the new track broke into the old one, making the going worse than ever. New tracks were continually being made, often leading one into another so that we hardly knew which one to take.

On the low tides, the water never came over this part of the marsh, so if the weather stayed sharp and dry, the tracks had time to harden up. This helped, but when the tides started to rise and the tracks were covered, we were in for trouble. Tractors were getting stuck almost every day. Trailers were going in up to their axles in mud, with the weight of the cockles, and many a time had to be unloaded so that we could dig them out. This delayed those following and they either had to muck in and help or wait until the way was clear.

Then came a day when we had the devil's own luck. One of the tractors which had been left out on the shore all night wouldn't start at any price. We tried towing it, we tried all we knew, but the engine refused to turn over. At last, we had to tow it off the marsh. That was a day lost for that chap, and hours of our time lost too — all because of the greed of a few, who wanted to be first out to get the lion's share.

Several of the men had gone on ahead and were busy gathering cockles; once we had got the broken-down tractor out of the way, the rest of us joined them. Soon the time came for us to make our way back as the tide was turning, and we had to call it a day. With our few bags of cockles, we were making for the shore when there was a sudden hold-up. As the first tractor raced ahead, not seeing that anything was wrong, the second had lurched to one side and stopped. The men were soon all shouting and cursing, frustrated after the trouble we had already gone through that day. Two of us scrambled along the muddy track, to find that the front wheel bearings had gone; the wheel had come off, and the cockle bags had slipped, strewing shellfish all over the place.

All we could do at that time of the day was to leave everything — tractor,cockles and all — where it was until the next morning. It was a good thing we were far enough up on the marsh to be above the tideline. In the morning we got back early and a farmer with hydraulic lifting gear on his tractor came to give us much-needed help. The axle of the damaged machine was buried deep in the mud; it took a good deal of cleaning before we could get the new bearings in and the wheel back on. Another crisis over!

Whereas in earlier years the fishermen of this area sold their catch themselves, now a lorry would come down to the shore, and each tractor unloaded its cockles as it came off the sands. Some of the men started leaving the cockle grounds early, to be first alongside the lorry, making sure their catch was taken. Some days we would get to the lorry, which was already piled high with bags of cockles, and the driver would shout, 'Can't take any more.' So it became a mad rush to get to the lorry with the catch. It was first come first served — if you were late, you would hear the driver shouting, 'Full up, have to take yours tomorrow.' This was what happened when the cockles became so plentiful. They were carted off for a very low price; if you objected the chap with the wagon could always find silly beggars who would step in and work for next to nothing.

Even at the best of times cockling was not easy work. It can only be described as hard graft. When there were plenty of cockles, they had to be dragged, that is raked up, as near to the jumbo as possible, while the sand was still in motion from the rocking of the jumbo. First, the cockles were raked in from the side of the beds: this was the hardest part, as you had to put your whole weight firmly on the rake, making sure the job was done properly, and not dragging the rake over the top of the shells so that they were broken.

Raking the cockles from the middle of the beds was slightly easier. As long as the fellow on the jumbo kept it swaying nicely away, water came up out of the sand and the cockles would roll along in the wet, without so much pressure being put on the rake. Then a few yards away the riddle was pushed into the heap of cockles, scooping up with a sharp shake all the smaller shellfish, hen-pennies, which are the small pink ones about the size of a fingernail. These would spoil the look of the cockles if they were left in. The 'wheaat' too was riddled out and left to grow on. Next, the cockles were shaken out of the riddle and into the basket — three baskets to the hundredweight. We always carried a spade to dig a hole, which soon filled with water to wash the cockles in before bagging them.

In cold weather cockles can be kept fresh for days before being boiled and eaten. In hot weather it is totally different, and they must be boiled as soon as you get them home; if they catch the heat of the sun, they open and the fish go sour in the shells.

All this really hard work and good fresh air gave us ravenous appetites, and we were ready for the good meal waiting for us at home. Anyone a bit faddy about his food only needed to be taken out working on the sands, and he would have eaten anything put in front of him. It would also have brought colour into his cheeks — to both ends, I would say, after a bumpy ride there and back on a tractor and trailer, over the rough, ridged sand.

Of course, not all the fishermen would be cockling. One or two would probably still be shrimping. Another might perhaps be occupied in setting a stake net out on a dyke foot for the white fluke, the catching of which made a welcome supplement to our income.

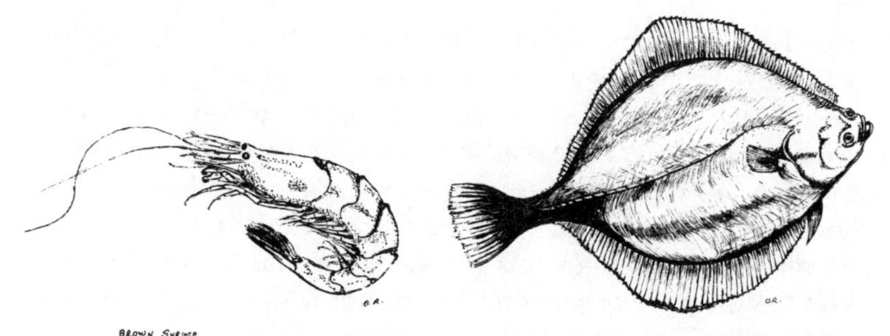

BROWN SHRIMP

WHITE FLUKE OR FLOUNDER.

The flukes, or flounders, which we catch in Morecambe Bay, are very tasty and can easily be mistaken for plaice, there being so slight a difference in taste between the two. The fluke is just a little coarser than the plaice, the latter having small orange-coloured spots on the upper side. It used to be easily picked out by the housewife when buying from the local market, but today many a good fluke may have similar markings to the plaice. This may suggest cross-breeding, but whereas the fluke can be caught well up in the estuaries, the plaice seems to prefer deeper and more open waters and is rarely caught very far up in the bay.

Stake nets are set out in the bay to trap the flukes. As the tide fills the bay, the flukes come up with it to their feeding grounds, which are the large areas of very young cockles and hen-pennies. These bivalves form their main diet when they are available. The flukes find their feeding ground, 'dooak' into the sand — that means they make a flopping movement to soften the sand — and sink down almost underneath it, probably moving on from time to time chewing up the shellfish as they go.

They are trapped on the ebb tide, in a number of different ways; in all the methods, stakes are put in about a yard apart, well down into the sand, with the nets attached to them. In some areas, when the tide has ebbed and you are able to get out on to the sand to fish the nets, the imprint of the flukes can often be seen. This is what we call 'a good show' meaning there are quite a number of flukes in the area, and it helps when you are looking for a good place to set your nets.

As soon as the hard frosts come, the flukes make their way down into deeper water, and do not return until the spring, around March. By this time they have spawned, and haven't much flesh on them. Given a few weeks they soon get back to their prime, but during this time they are best left alone.

In the meantime, there is salmon fishing, which runs from spring into summer. The season for this, up here in Morecambe Bay, is from 1 April to 31 August. In years gone by there was no allocation of licences for catching salmon as there is today, so poaching was done in quite a big way. Poaching does still go on today, as the price of salmon rockets, but with the stiff increase in fines, people are less likely to take part in what could well be a losing battle.

The method the poachers used was to stand in the shallows on a sand bar, with a long-handled garden fork, the prongs of which had been straightened by the local blacksmith. Used with skill, this was a lethal weapon, as the number of salmon taken showed. Speed played a great part in successfully catching the salmon as it made its way through the shallows. There would be a line of perhaps a dozen men, all with forks at the ready, and when the salmon showed, it was every man for himself. I've heard Dad say that on more than one occasion the fork had not gone through the fish, but through someone's foot!

Dad was in on this and was an expert at catching salmon in this way. Times were often very hard, and it was the only way of making a living. I remember Mam and Dad taking me on the train, with a big pram full of salmon. They had it covered up so that it looked like a baby in the pram. I am sure the guard thought there was something fishy going on! The salmon was sold to a wet fish shop in Ulverston, and I well remember the pram bumping along the old cobbled street.

There were water bailiffs then, just as there are today. Sometimes Dad and his mates were chased mile upon mile across the sands, but, knowing the area and the shoreline as they did, they were able to outwit their pursuers, often hiding their catch in the hedgerows or in a turnip field and returning at night or in the early hours of the morning to collect the salmon.

Later on, the fishing authorities decided to issue licences to a number of fishermen, and Dad, along with several other mates, got one. But they were no longer able to catch fish in the old way, with a fork. They had to use a lave net, very long in the beam, like the ones used by the fishermen in that well-known

salmon river, the Lune. These were not a success, as the currents in the River Kent are much stronger than in the Lune, so a different design of net had to be used, with a much smaller beam. It needed to be of a manageable size, to enable the fishermen to run with it and have perfect control. He would get in front of the fish and then scoop it up out of the water. This was a far better way than using a fork, and less hazardous.

A recent development is the fishing of whitebait, the small, silvery baby herrings. Until a few years ago, the fishermen of this area knew nothing about them, being introduced to them by a Morecambe fisherman; now the whitebait have become a seasonal catch on this side of the bay, following on after the shrimps and flukes have gone down into deeper water for the winter. Ideal conditions for catching whitebait are sharp, frosty weather, with little or no wind to scatter the shoals of these tiny fish.

Large nets are set on the sands with guide ropes running from them to iron bars which hold the nets in position. Floats are attached to the front of each net, along the top cord; when the tide comes in, they lift the cord to the surface of the water, keeping the net open at the mouth. On the turn of the tide, the whitebait swim into the nets, where the long tail ends of very small mesh trap the fish. These nets must be fished as early as possible, otherwise the gulls peck the fish, breaking the flesh and ruining them.

A very cold, tedious and thankless job is the preparation of the whitebait once you have got your catch home. This small fish has to be tipped into cold water as soon as possible after being brought into the fish house. Imagine a cold December evening, with something very good on the television; all the family, especially the younger ones, have been looking forward to it, sitting around a cosy log fire. Then, in comes Dad in his waders. 'Now, you lot, a good catch of whitebait, but I can't manage all these on my own. I'll need your help.' A sudden silence. They all know what to expect as they have done it all before. I ask my daughter Jean to ring my parents, Nana and Grandad Rob, as they are always called. They really like this job of sorting the whitebait and have been disappointed many a time when catches have been poor and we have finished the sorting without their help.

Coming outside to the fish house from the fireside, is bad enough, but sorting the whitebait means having a flow of cold water cascading over the fish all the time while we are picking out bits of seaweed, small round jellyfish and the odd shrimp. There will often be a few sprats too. All the waste is taken back to the sands for the birds. This may be a miserably uncomfortable process but it is the only way we can make sure of leaving the whitebait clean.

Although we have two paraffin heaters in the building, the nights are so cold that everyone's hands are freezing after sorting the fish for a short time. There is ample room round the white formica-topped table, but it is virtually impossible to keep dry, however hard you try.

Once a good number of fish are clean, they are put on perforated trays to drain before being weighed and then packed in plastic bags and put into waxed cardboard boxes ready to be frozen. Next day I take the whole catch, boxed and frozen, to the factory at Flookburgh. A good catch can mean several or all of the family being out in the fish house, sorting and packing, for five or six hours at a stretch, because these small fish cannot be left. They have to be packed within the shortest time possible or they begin to deteriorate.

Although I am always pleased to get a good catch, I am more than pleased when, at the end of the day, with the last of the fish packed and in the freezers, and my last job of clearing up and swilling down completed, we can all go indoors, have a hot drink and go to bed. But first, I must put my wet clothes and my thigh boots in front of the fire to dry, ready to be off out to the sands first thing in the morning.

5 Shrimping with Tractors

Looking back, it seems that the traditional ways of fishing in Morecambe Bay were bound to come to an end. The use of tractors and lorries was increasing and now, one or two of the fishermen hit on a new idea: shrimping with tractors. They had been used on and off for years, but only for cockling, never for shrimping because none of us thought we could ever get into the depth of water we trawled with the horse and cart. Horses get used to the water; and when going in deep and dropping out of their depth they can easily swim along until their feet touch the bottom again, but tractors and water don't agree at all.

We tried first in some of the shallow dykes at low tides. Towing a trailer with the shrimp net fastened behind, we could get a fair catch, but one thing we noticed was that with the speed of the tractor, as against that of the horse and cart, we were getting into the water too soon after the tide had ebbed and the channels were too deep. Tractors were so insensitive too. With a horse, you could pull on the rope of your net and you would know what sort of a catch you had in it. If your nets were full of muck, the horse would have slackened speed and you could pull out. The tractor just went blindly on at the same speed and you would have no idea what was going on in the nets. Tractors couldn't tell you as the horse would have done, when something went wrong. Your beams could be broken, your nets ripped to pieces — I've had this happen to me many a time. There's a lot of heartbreak working with tractors on the sands.

At first we thought it was grand. We had wasted no time getting to the fishing grounds, and we were home in no time. We thought, 'This is progress.' But we had some really sad 'do's', some really weary days. We would trawl down, then pull out and find the nets full of sludge and seaweed; as soon as we stopped, the flow of the water through the nets would stop too. The nets would drop to the bottom, and the sand built up on it, holding it fast in the channel bed. Then we would have to dig the net out and it would be torn to pieces. That meant the end of shrimping for that day: quite a big loss.

We had all this to learn. We did not do so badly until more tractors came out on to the sands. Then there were some ten to fifteen fishermen out with their tractors, all towing trailers. If it was new ground, no one wanted to be first but everyone wanted to be second, and of course no one wanted to be the last! You can imagine what a muddle it was. Some of the men got really difficult; there would be cursing and swearing, and they would even ram your trailer at times. We were getting in each other's way all the time, with tractors being forced into deep water and having to be towed out. It was almost useless to try and fish under these conditions. At night it was even worse. We had the bright idea of using torches to signal our intentions to each other, but the torches would refuse to function or would be lost altogether. Sometimes the wrong number of flashes was given causing confusion, so we gave up that idea.

Some of us then tried building a platform, three to four feet high, on the chassis of an old taxi. These were bought from a scrap merchant who would cut off all the bodywork, leaving just the chassis, the four wheels and the steering column. We had metal struts welded upright on to the chassis, and on this fixed a wooden platform to carry the nets, and also for a man to ride on. A drawbar was welded on the front of the chassis so that we could pull it with the tractor. We made the platform so that the man on top could steer in and out of the water, and manoeuvre when looking for the best places for shrimps.

At this early stage, our ideas for manning the trailer were unsuccessful, being based on our experience with horse and cart. On our first attempts, the tractor driver would slacken off speed, when we were ready to haul in the nets, until the engine was just turning the wheels; this gave the man on the trailer a chance to haul in each net separately, tip his catch of shrimps into the boxes, and then drop the nets off the back of the trailer, one at a time, into the water. The tractor driver would then open up the throttle and gather up to his normal trawling speed. While the trailer was in deep water, the man on it could lift the nets on quite easily because of buoyancy. Once the trailer came to the side of the water, where it was shallower, it was hard work to haul in the nets: having to lift them this great distance worked against you, as the nets could be heavily laden with seaweed as well as a good weight of shrimps.

We also found that when the trailer dropped into a hole, the fisherman had no way of attracting the attention of the tractor driver. The noise of the tractor made shouting useless, and he ended up holding on like grim death, in danger of being thrown off or half drowned when the trailer went down into deeper water. No lives were lost, but before something really dangerous did happen, we needed to think this one out. Maybe we could lower the trailer so that the platform just cleared the wheels; or perhaps the trailer should not be manned after all.

A couple of mornings later we had managed to make the alterations to lower the platform and decided to have a try-out the next day. I looked at the tide table, and it was pretty early going next morning.There would be other tractors out on the sands in different areas, but I thought that it would be better, since this was our first attempt, to have a particular spot to ourselves — just Bill and me with our tractor, and Bob, my mate at the time, with his. So I told Bill, 'I'll away up village an' see Bob an' tell him what time we'll be settin' off in t'mornin'.' Bob agreed with the plan, saying, 'If tha's up before me, give us a knock, Ced.' I am pretty good at getting up, but I set the alarm, just in case, and we went to bed.

Up next morning; it wasn't quite daylight. The kettle was on, a bit of breakfast made, and Bill came down; we had a drink of tea, then out to put one or two boxes on the tractor. A few last-minute checks, and I went to see if Bob was up. He had a light, so I just tapped on the door. 'Aw reet,' he shouted.

We gave him about half an hour and then we started the tractor up. We had arranged to meet at six-thirty. Bob followed us as we made our way down the marsh. We stopped a few minutes, as we always did with the horse and cart, to have a natter to find out whether we were going to the west or to the east, or straight out towards Morecambe. It all depended on which way the wind was blowing. This particular morning, it was best, we thought, for the spot known as Cod 'oller. This was the same spot we called the 'goldmine' when we were shrimping, as there would always be well-filled boxes after a 'do' up there. So it was off, after another check over the tractors and trailers.

'Can I drive now, Dad?' Bill was all excitement at this new venture, so I said, 'Aye, Bill, thee get on but don't drive so damn fast. Take thi' time now, cos it's different riding on a tractor than it is driving a horse and cart. These bracks, tha can come across a dyke so sharp, an' if tha drops down yan o' these, tractor can be easily overturned. So, as it's first time, Bill, just take thi' time.'

'Aw reet' — and with that we set off, Bob following close behind. It seemed to take us no time at all before we could see the 'goldmine'. What a difference to going with a horse and cart. We had a few dykes to cross and there was quite a westerly breeze; it was a real nice morning. Lights were showing as we set off, and drawing towards the 'gold-mine' we came to a big breast and what we call a drop-off. The sands are not flat from one end to the other; there are many variations in the levels out there, and we were going on a right big high bank, and looking down at the place where we were going to shrimp, which was in a very low area.

At the water's edge, we separated, Bill and I going ahead about a hundred yards before we stopped. Now we had to unhitch the tractor from the trailer, so I pulled the pin out and shouted, 'Aw reet, Bill, pull away.' He drove the tractor round and out on to the side; Bob had to do the same with his own, as he had no one to help him on this particular morning. But there was no hurry as there were only our two tractors out. Bill jumped down from the tractor, and helped me to get our nets off the trailer, pulling them right back to make ready for off. We waited until Bob had his nets unloaded too.

Now for it. There was the big coil of wire rope on the trailer, and this had to come out evenly; it was no use trying to get it off too quickly because it could easily get tangled, and then we could be half the tide trying to get it untangled again. Bill climbed back on the tractor. 'Just take it out slowly, Bill.' He seemed to be doing all right, but at the last few yards I put my hand up to stop him before he got too far. The last few coils I pulled off cautiously with my hands: I didn't want any spikes of wire sticking in my fingers. I waved to Bill to drive back over the wire, but he seemed to be a long time coming back. Then I realised that he had some wire rope caught around the tractor wheels.

Bill had already got down to try and sort things out. He had turned too sharply, and the treads on the back wheel had picked up the wire and wound it a few times round the back axle before he saw what was happening. Anyhow, he's a bright lad, is Bill, and he soon got the wire free: he had to keep getting off and pulling the wire under the tread, and then backing over it. We found out that day that when you turned you had to make sure that the wire lay between the tractor wheels. Bill should have reversed his tractor just a little further before turning to come back to me; then the wire would have been lying loosely on the sand, not taut and so liable to be picked up by the large treads of the rear wheels.

While all this had been going on, the tide had ebbed. We had stopped on the water's edge but now we were out on the dry sand. Bob was ready, so I said to Bill, 'Run out, and when tha gets to t'last few yards, get into very low gear and set off slowly.' There wasn't likely to be a lot of movement in this water where we were going to trawl; by this time the water had gone out at least fifty yards. We had nets out, and had run the wire out and hitched it to the tractor: everything was perfect now. Since the new idea was not to have a man riding on the trailer, we just turned the steering wheel slightly towards the water and tied it tight, so it couldn't move. I hadn't to turn the wheels too far, as this would be putting too much strain on the tractor, if I had left them straight, the trailer would just have followed the tractor, instead of veering into the water. This would mean a wasted 'do'.

Bob stood on the side of the channel and said,'I'll let thee be goin', Ced.'

'Right, Bob, I'll away an' walk in front.' Bill set off slowly and the trailer veered away out into the water and finally disappeared. Bob gave us a hundred yards' start, then he too drove off and his trailer went into the water in fine style. Just then, I noticed some seaweed along the edge of the channel. We weren't going to trawl too far down for this first time, but this made up our minds for us. Seaweed was littered everywhere. The water was full of it. I turned round and waved to the others to pull out. Now we had to turn the tractors at right angles to the channel, and gradually the trailers came up out of the water. First of all the drawbar appeared, just like the snorkel of a submarine, then the steering wheel. Then the nets, which were several feet behind the trailer, began to lift above the water, which was ebbing fast. 'We'll 'ave to be getting t'nets on, Bill.' I turned back and walked along the sand, skirting round one or two soft patches. Bob was just pulling out. 'There's nah tellin' what weights we 'ave.' With horse and cart, of course, you could tell when you had a heavy net, as the horse would slacken speed.

We found we had a very good catch of shrimps, 'good tails', as we say. They were so heavy, I shouted to Bill to come and give me a hand. 'Give 'em a good swashin', Bill.' He got hold of the tail of the net while I held it a bit higher up, and we swilled the shrimps in the water until they were pretty clear of sand. 'Now, heave 'em up.' We swung the heavy net up on to the back of the trailer and I untied the tope to let the shrimps pour into the box. 'Nice shrimps these,' I said as I ran my hand through them. 'By gum, Bill, I was lucky there!' An attapile, the dreaded weaver fish, was squirming about in among the shrimps. The sting of this fish is so terrible, I've seen grown men cry with the pain it inflicts. 'It's always risky to run your 'and through t'shrimps, Bill, and if tha does get stung, t'only thing tha can do for a bit o' relief is to piddle on it! So watch out for 'em.'

Bob was just getting his nets on, so I went down to give him a hand. 'Not a bad do, Ced, I've a couple of good tails. Give us a hand up with 'em, will yer?' We swashed them and got them clean, and then up they went and were soon emptied into the boxes. 'Better get tails tied, Bob, or it won't be a good do next trip! I've made that mistake mesel' once or twice, and had a wasted trawl.' The tail is the narrow funnel end of the shrimp net into which the whole catch of shrimps is gathered. A thin short piece of rope is used here, fastened securely before each trawl; it must not be too close to the end, otherwise it might work its way loose as it drags along the sea bed, which would mean a trawl wasted. When emptying the catches of shrimps, the tail-end of the net is lifted into the boxes and the rope unfastened, releasing the catch.

We were well satisfied with our first trawl, although Bob had not had as long a wire as us, so hadn't gone in quite so far, and his shrimps were just that little bit smaller than ours. But now the tide had ebbed and on the next trawl we would be able to go much farther in and get much bigger shrimps. Bill had been picking bits of seaweed out of the boxes of shrimps, and I went back to him and told him we would do another trawl.

Now we had to get back to where we started the first time. This meant we had to run back over the wire, but Bill had learnt from the first tangle and did the job quite well. We tried going a little bit faster, as otherwise we wouldn't have enough time for a last trawl. We left the rope out at its full length, and when we turned the tractor, the trailer swung round — it must have been going all of forty miles an hour! What an experience this was. The long wire kept biting into the sand, and it would pull on the back of the tractor, making it lurch so that you felt it would tip over. But whatever speed the trailer was going, as soon as it hit the water it stopped.

We had to keep our distance from one another, as we could see the danger of a trailer hurtling by at the end of two hundred yards of wire rope. It wasn't too bad when there were only two tractors, but imagine the chaos with ten, fifteen and sometimes twenty tractors roving about on the sands, all swinging their trailers round at a 'rate of knots'! There was a near-tragedy once when a chap misjudged his distance and swung his trailer round hitting ours just below the front wheels. Bill and I, luckily, were standing on the trailer at the time sorting out shrimps; we were both knocked over and severely jolted, but no other damage was done. If I had been standing at the side of the trailer, as I was only minutes before, I would have had my legs cut clean off.

By the time we finished our trawls, we were satisfied with our morning's work. There were several tractors out shrimping as there are three or four places where you can get shrimps, but they had gone over to the other side of the bay. They couldn't have done quite as well as us. Later we had a good long session boiling, and no doubt there were a few eyes on our boiler house.

You can't keep anything to yourself in a village. As fishermen pass one another they might say, 'Look yer, Ced's still boilin' — 'e must 'a done weel.' They see steam rising for longer than usual and put two and two together; then, when you take your shrimps out to the pickers, it soon gets round that you had a good catch. The word spreads, as everybody knows everybody else — and they know everybody's business too!

So they had found out that we had done well, and we were in for a surprise when we got down to the marsh the following morning. There were half a dozen tractors, like dots on the horizon. They had followed our tracks and were on the way to Cod 'oller! 'This is a bugger,' I thought. Anyhow, we tipped our husks out for the gulls on the edge of the marsh, as we usually do. Bill was driving my tractor and Bob came up behind us. Rather than try and catch them up, we decided to take our own time. The six had already got their nets off and had their trailers in the water. I knew they were too early, much too early for that area. They wouldn't be able to get in deep enough. We had set off an hour later than on the previous morning.

It was wet this morning, with a wind blowing the rain, and when you're driving a tractor out there, rain hits your face like bullets. So I said to Bill, 'Take yer time, let them be going.' He ran the wire out nicely, did Bill, and at the same time I lifted the nets off the trailer, put them out on to the sand and then went to give my mate a hand. When we were ready, I shouted,'All right now, Bill, into low gear and away we'll go quietly.' I was going to walk down the side, as it gets cold sitting on the tractor.

The morning before had been such a good one, but today rain was lashing and wind blowing. This is how we find it out on Morecambe Bay. Change can come suddenly; you have to be ready for any sort of weather. I could see the chaps in front were all pulling out after their first trawl; they had their nets on and had tipped their shrimps. Then I saw one after another having a look at the catch of this one and that one. If they'd had a good catch, they wouldn't have been doing that: they wouldn't have been able to get their nets in quickly enough, and they would soon have been back down the side to start a second trawl. As we watched them they seemed to be having a discussion, and before we got near they had run their nets out again and were carrying on, going down. When we got to their marks on the sand, I could see a bit of muck on the side, and I thought, we're not going down there. The seaweed had been thick down there yesterday and I couldn't see it being much cleaner today, so I waved Bill out, and Bob followed suit. 'I've two good tails 'ere,' Bob shouted. 'Like a cow's belly! Give us a hand to get em on, will yer, Ced.'

'Aye, ours are t'same, we can't better that,' I told him as we heaved the heavy catch on to the back of the trailer and tipped them into the boxes. 'Good big 'uns an' all. That lot 'll not be doin' much good. They'll 'ave their nets full o' weed afore they've gone 'alf a mile!'

I thought, 'Now it'll be best for us if those lads in front carry on where they are,' but I could see that they were just pulling out. They were looking our way and must have decided to come and have a 'do' near us. There they were, all six of them getting their nets on. I could see the trailers flying round, one after the other, and they were making along the sands towards us. Not wanting to be pushed out by that lot, I said to Bill, 'Come on, Bill, we mustn't waste time.' I got him round and he drove off in the opposite direction. Then I went to help Bob, and got his nets off while he ran his wire out. Just as Bob got his trailer into the water, the six tractors came up. Another minute or two and they would have gone past Bob's net and he would have been snookered. He would have had to wait for the six of them to start trawling before he could have got into the water. The day before, with just our two tractors, we could take our time, but with six more coming into the channel where we were working, it was going to be quite hectic and we had to have our wits about us all the time. The first tractors get the best catch, so of course they pull out and get back quickly to be first down the next time. It becomes very dangerous.

This would be our last trawl, as the tide had turned and the tracks we had made while trawling when the tide was ebbing, which had shown plainly like a smooth road across the sand, were now being covered by the oncoming tide. Bill pulled out until the trailer was well clear of the water, and by the time we had got the nets on, the water was already washing round our feet. We had been able to wash the shrimps, but left them in the nets, as we always did with our last catch. Now, the trailer had to be hitched to the tractor and the two hundred yards of wire rope coiled on to the back of the trailer. With Bill's help, I made short work of this, but Bob, being on his own, needed assistance. We saw that the other six tractors were now making for the marsh, so we started off and were soon on the road home.

The journey back was much quicker with a tractor than it had been with the horse and cart, and at first we found we were getting back before the boiler fire had been lit. The fire was usually laid early, ready for a match to be put to it as soon as the horse's hooves were heard clattering along the road. Then the water would be boiling by the time we had unloaded and had a meal. Now that we got home so much sooner we had to reorganise the fire-lighting. That wasn't the only difference. We were bringing home much bigger catches and the boiling took that much longer. The quality of the shrimps was very good too, and this brought more and more fishermen on to the sands.

Even with our improved methods, fishing with a tractor could be dangerous. The sands were as treacherous as ever, as Bill and I found out when shrimping one evening. Bill drove while I walked on in front, as he didn't know the sands too well. The channel was running down the shore, round the Headland and making back towards Silverdale. There were a few melgraves in the side of the banking. Melgraves are holes which have been scoured out by the incoming tide; then, on the ebb tide, sand is deposited in these holes, and it is very soft, like a kind of quicksand. We kept well clear of these areas, and when we got about a quarter of a mile farther down, the sand seemed to level out.

It was just coming dusk, and when I looked round, I could vaguely make out a chap waving his arms about for help. Seemingly, he had taken his tractor a little bit farther in than us. We were following the side of the channel and he had gone into the water to try to get his nets clear of ours. By doing this, he had gone into quicksands. By the time we had pulled out, hauled our nets on to the back of the trailer and gone back to him, all that was showing of his tactor was the exhaust and a little bit of the steering wheel! It was a goner! The trailer was stuck out in the middle of the channel with the nets sanded, because as soon as you stop, the fast-flowing river piles sand on to the nets and they are anchored so fast with the weight of the sand that it is quite impossible to recover them. We tried to pull the trailer out with a wire to my tractor, but we couldn't move it. We could do nothing at all about his tractor. It was too far under the sand. It was pitch dark by this time and we had to leave it. All we could do was to give the poor fellow a lift home. It was a big loss for him. He had lost everything. That tractor is still there . . . under the sand.

As the number of fishermen, and the size of the catches, increased, the consequences of fishing with tractors began to be felt. First new bye-laws had to be made. A sea fishery officer was appointed who had a good knowledge of the Morecambe Bay area. He was fitted up with a tractor so that he could keep track of what was going on. Before this, when the horse and cart were still used for fishing, he had to walk. He would have had all the exercise he needed trying to keep an eye on all the people gathering cockles or shrimping. He had his job to do just as we had. He would come up to us and take out his rule and measure the jumbo, if we were cockling. This had to be the regulation 4ft 6in long. Shrimp nets were measured at the tail end. The length of the beam had to be 13ft 6in. The mesh was also measured: this must not be too small. Some crafty fishermen would put their new nets into a mixture and shrink them, so as to catch more than anyone else. A tractor was allowed to tow two nets, but sometimes a fisherman would not be satisfied, and would fasten a third net on to the towing wire, so that it ran on ground just clear of the other two; he knew of course that this was illegal.

I was shrimping one day, along with several others, when the chap in front of me was using three nets. Suddenly, out of the blue, coming towards us on his tractor were the fishery officer and his superiors. They pulled alongside me, asked how we were doing, took a look at my shrimps and remarked how good they were, and stayed along with us for quite a while. Little did they know the tractor in front of me was running three nets! As long as the nets remained in the water, they were out of sight. At last something made the men decide to move on. Was I glad!

If we had come to an area full of seaweed and so on, we would have had to haul our nets and the culprit would have been in dire trouble. But they seemed well satisfied with the answers we had given to their questions, and that was the end of it. All for the best, we thought, as we saw them making for the shore.

Meanwhile, trawling with two nets and sometimes three, to each tractor, with the wire ropes dragging on the sand, day in and day out, was doing as much damage to the shrimps as if the whole area were lined with nets. Now, manilla rope is used instead of wire for towing the trailer; being light in weight, it floats, and so does not disturb the young shrimps and flatfish as the wire rope does. I fear, though, that too much damage has already been done over the years, through this and over-fishing, for cockling and shrimping ever to be worthwhile as a full-time job again.

It is my belief that although the Morecambe Bay area has in the past been a prolific breeding place for fish, the area where the rivers enter the bay are now becoming more and more unproductive. We used to find huge areas of wheaat and knew that in a few years they would be keeping the cockling going. Mussels too were found in large numbers, big juicy mussels which we used to gather with a very long pronged rake; these too have disappeared, along with the periwinkles. All these were wholesome foods which in the past provided many a family with a good cheap meal.

As catches grew poorer, and seasons very much later in starting, some of the tradesmen who had been fishing for a number of years decided to leave the sands and go back to their own jobs. Bob too went off to a factory where he could earn better money, leaving Bill and me on our own. But I, and those like me, who have spent a lifetime on the sands, have to stick it out through thick and thin. We have known no other way of life but fishing.

Cockling in Morecambe Bay: the technique is basically the same today as when this photograph was taken a hundred years or more ago. The horse has been loosed from the shafts of the cart and wrapped up well to keep him warm while the family gather fish; the son is rocking the jumbo, while his mother flicks the cockles into her basket with a cramb

Another cockling party. The traditional cockle basket and riddle are seen very clearly in the foreground

Main Street, Flookburgh, showing my parents' cottage just to the right of the old water pump. Note the fishermen's carts drawn up outside the cottages. Apart from the invasion of the motor car, little has changed in the village to this day

Fishing the trap nets for white flukes. On the left is my son Paul

Heading and gutting the flukes for market. *Left to right*, my daughter Jean and a friend, my wife Olive, and Dad

Emptying the tails after fishing for whitebait

Surveying a gulley, while the walkers wait on high ground to be given the 'all clear'

A large party of walkers fording the Kent channel

Looking out across the route shortly to be taken by the drilling tower under my guidance

PART TWO
GUIDE TO THE SANDS

TO ALL TO WHOM these Presents shall come GREETING WHEREAS the power of appointing and removing the Guide over Kent Sands in the County Palatine of Lancaster is vested in Her Majesty in right of Her Duchy of Lancaster And WHEREAS the Office of the said Guide over Kent Sands is now vacant NOW I THE RIGHT HONOURABLE IAIN NORMAN MACLEOD Chancellor of Her Majesty's Duchy and County Palatine of Lancaster by virtue of all powers enabling me in that behalf DO HEREBY APPOINT as from the first day of October One thousand nine hundred and sixty three CEDRIC ROBINSON of 12 Jutland Avenue, Ravenstown, Flookburgh in the County Palatine aforesaid Guide over the said Kent Sands TO HAVE hold occupy and exercise the said Office during the pleasure of the Chancellor of the Duchy for the time being performing such duties and receiving such emoluments as may be assigned to the said Office by the Trustees for the time being under a Scheme of the Charity Commissioners dated the Nineteenth day of May One thousand eight hundred and eighty two or any subsequent modification thereof.

DATED this Seventeenth day of October 1963.

Iain Macleod

6 Guide's Farm

In the early sixties came a change which affected the lives of all my family, as well as adding new interest to my own way of life out on the sands. I heard that at Grange-over-Sands the guide was giving up his post, and that if I was interested in the job I would have to apply in writing. At a later date, I was asked to go for an interview and I was finally chosen for the job of Queen's Guide to the Sands of Morecambe Bay, in the year 1963, when my daughter Jean was just nine months old.

There are in fact two officially appointed guides, one for each side of the bay. The River Kent is my responsibility, while the other guide, Mr Butler, is responsible for the Leven Sands. The Kent crossing is normally done from the Morecambe side of the bay to Grange, a distance of between eight and twelve miles; it affords beautiful panoramic views and is by far the most popular walk. A shorter version, from Grange to Arnside, is arranged from time to time. The Leven crossing, for which my colleague is appointed, is not so well known. About three and a half miles in length, it takes a line from Flookburgh to Canal Foot, near Ulverston. (For the routes of the walks, see the map on page 24.

Although local tradition has it that the guides were in existence in the time of King John, there is no evidence to support this. The office of Guide over the Kent Sands may have been instituted by the prior of Cartmel, the religious house nearest to the sands, in the fourteenth century, but there are no records to be found of guides before the reign of Henry VIII.

The salaries of both guides are secured from the revenues of the Duchy of Lancaster, yet by the Charitable Acts of 1853 and 1869 they passed under the control of the Charity Commissioners, with the Chancellor of the Duchy one of the trustees. In 1882 the Chancellor was discharged from this responsibility and three local trustees were appointed to administer the charity. This arrangement is still in force. The guide's salary is £15 a year, paid to him quarterly after rent has been deducted; obviously it is not a full-time job, and the bulk of my income still comes from my fishing. Although we pay rates on the house which goes with the job, we have the use of the adjoining land, with its outbuildings, and the property is kept in repair by the trustees.

The appointment meant that we had to move to Grange from our home in Ravenstown, a small village just a hop, skip and a jump from Flookburgh where my parents had lived for most of their lives. At this stage, we were still boiling our shrimps at Dad's cottage, as there was no suitable place where we were living.

We moved to Guide's Farm in early October, and found we had a lot to do to make ourselves comfortable. We had to work night and day, as it was just in the busiest time for the shrimping. One big drawback was that there was no electricity supply to Guide's Farm. There was gas lighting, but only in the living room and the kitchen, and anyway the light was so dull and poor that it was not even as good as the glow from a candle. My wife Olive now had extra burdens thrown on her, with five children and a husband to wash, cook and iron for, and no washing machine, electric iron and vacuum cleaner. We could not use our cooker or television. It was very hard, but we were willing to put up with these things for a time at least.

With everyone doing their bit to help, we eventually made headway. Decorating was a task we all shared, but as it was so late on in the year, the days were short and it came in dark just after teatime, which didn't help us in any way!

We used two oil lamps with mantles, and these gave us a much better light than the gas in the living room, though as they hung from the low beams I was forever banging my head on them. Candles were used to light us up to bed, and we were always very careful with them, because the house was so very old. Many a time, getting up in the middle of the night to go out shrimping, I found out how I missed the electricity. I had to use a torch to see the time by my bedside clock; I couldn't be fiddling about with matches in the middle of the night. I got up and went downstairs, and then had to light a Primus stove, which we had borrowed, before I could have a cup of tea. This was going back to the olden days, with all their disadvantages.

The house has an interesting history. It is said that Oliver Cromwell once slept there, and as I made my way down the creaking stairs, in the very early hours, with the sound of the winter winds howling round the house, I could almost feel that I had seen him. I would often think about how the people dressed, so many centuries ago, and sometimes even imagined that our old house was haunted. At one time, long ago, the upper floor was one big room: travellers crossing the sands late at night, tired and weary from the long journey, often very wet and cold, could come into Guide's Farm and get a few hours' rest — and a drink of something to 'warm the cockles of their hearts', as the house had been granted a licence to sell them ale. This, in those long ago days, augumented the guide's income; I could to with something of this nature today!

When Guide's Farm was built — and it is said to be about seven or eight hundred years old — the very high tides would probably have come right up into the house. There was no embankment to keep the tide at bay until the railway was built along the coast here. We found that all the ground floor sloped towards the shore, so the living rooms, with their old stone flag floors, could easily have been swilled out after such happenings. Oddly enough, there was a deep step into the kitchen, and the ceiling was so low that there was hardly enough headroom for anyone of my height — almost six feet — to stand upright. So we decided to dig up the floor and bring it level with the living room floors, as it was a danger in the poor light. Under the floor we found good clean sand and cockle shells, so it must have been tidal ground before being built on.

It seemed a very long winter to us, and as time passed, we were looking towards the day when we could have electricity brought to the house. We had been using oil lamps and candles for almost six months, although it seemed much longer; we had written to the trustees who appointed me, to see if it would be possible to have electricity installed, and they had given us the go-ahead, although we had to foot the bill in the first place. The money was paid back to us at a later date. We applied to the Electricity Board and soon things got moving. A gang of twelve men arrived to dig along the lane to Guide's Farm.

All was excitement when, in February 1964, the work was finished, and in March the current was turned on. This changed all our lives, but none so much as my wife's. The washer, fridge and cooker were soon fixed up in the kitchen, and made life really worth living again when it came to all the jobs Olive had to do for the whole family. All the fearsome shadows which had scared us for the last six months on the creaking staircase vanished, and going to bed was no longer a nightmare. Had we all been imagining those sinister figures lurking in the corners? The click of a switch, and they just disappeared. Even so, when I get up in the night to go to my nets, I step out on to the old, creaking landing and sometimes think I see a figure standing there. I say to myself, 'It can't be, Ced,' but I am always glad to get the light on.

We were very pleased with the progress we had made, and everything ran smoothly for several months. Then came a setback. As the house was so old, it had no damp course. Now all our hard work at wallpapering, of which we were so proud, was wasted: suddenly, piece by piece, the paper started coming away from the walls. We realised just how damp they were, and decided to strip off all the old plaster and start from rock bottom, making a really good job of it, plastering afresh. One night, we were sitting round a cheerful log fire when all at once there was a deafening roar. You would have thought a bomb had just dropped on the house. We rushed to open the sitting-room door. Olive was the first to see the mess. All the plaster we had put on had left the walls and was spread all over the carpet; there was dust and plaster everywhere. Olive was in tears. 'Never mind, love,' I said. 'We'll soon have it cleaned up, and then we'll see what can be done.'

We decided if we couldn't cure the damp, we would just have to hide it, so Robert, who was serving his apprenticeship as a joiner made battons on which he fastened hardboard, and we then papered over it. After this treatment the sitting room looked nice and cosy, but even then, when there was a heavy rain, some signs of damp would show. Eventually we put tarred paper on the walls of the ground-floor rooms, under the wallpaper, and this helped to stop the discoloration to some extent, though it did not prevent the dampness.

A year after this, we had an even greater shock. One evening, Olive was busy getting the children ready for bed. I had already gone upstairs, as I had to be out at four o'clock the next morning. I was just dozing off when I heard her shouting, 'Ced, Ced, come quick, there's a flood!'

It had rained steadily for some hours, and as I stepped down from the bedroom on to the landing I found I was ankle deep in water, which was running down the stairs like a waterfall. Olive was already lifting the lino from the living-room floor; as the floor slopes down towards the front door, the water was running out like a river. It bubbled up through the bottom stair as if there was a spring underneath. Upstairs in the bathroom, the lino was afloat. There was water seeping into the sitting room, and we had to move all the furniture and take up the carpet, which later had to go away to be dried. Water was running through the wall of the kitchen and had built up to about a foot deep outside the window. What a job we had to try to get everything out. There wasn't much sleep for any of us that night.

The house is built into the hillside, with earth reaching up to the foot of the kitchen window, and there is a door on the first-floor landing level with the ground outside. So it was not surprising that in really heavy rain, such as we had that day, the water should have built up sufficiently to flood the house. The trustees of the Duchy of Lancaster decided that the only way to prevent this from happening again would be to have the earth removed from most of the back wall of the house, and have it all cemented. This was done and fortunately it has proved very effective.

Meanwhile my appointment as guide at a fairly young age seemed to have aroused some interest further afield. In the spring of 1964, shortly after moving to Guide's Farm, I was visited by someone from BBC Radio. They wanted me to do a short talk on the cross-bay walks, with the sound of the sea birds and the howling winds picked up in the distance.

We went out on to the shore and found a secluded spot among some bushes, where we could be hidden from the wary eyes of the birds. The equipment was set up, and after they had explained what they wanted me to do, the recording started. All went well, although I felt a little bit nervous at first as this was the first time I had ever done anything like this. But I just talked of some of the walks and the people who had taken part in them, and quite forgot that a recording was being made. Afterwards everyone went back to our house for a hot drink and we were told when the programme would be broadcast.

On the night, all was excitement, as the whole family and several friends came in to hear the broadcast. There were so many in our living room that we had to sit two to a chair, and then some of us had to sit on the floor. At last, everyone fell silent as Olive said, 'Any minute now Dad will be on.' The children kept very quiet; you could have heard a pin drop. Then the programme was announced, followed by my broadcast. It seemed to be over in a very short time, but everyone thought it most interesting.

Following this, several journalists, reporters and writers came to see me from time to time, these visits followed by reports and pictures in a number of newspapers and magazines, both locally and far afield. One excellent picture, taken by one of the walkers, showed me leading a very long string of walkers through the river, and this appeared in the *Geographical Magazine*.

In February 1967, I helped BBC Television with a Morecambe Bay film for the 'Look North' programme, and again at the end of July 1974, was involved in a series called 'Lakeland Summer', which was shown on 'Pebble Mill at One'. I took part in the making of the film, leading a coach and a pair of horses over the sands in my role as guide; this time, though, I was on horseback, as in the old days. The programme was transmitted in October of that year, and must have created some interest, as it was repeated on BBC 2 in the following April.

On the television programme 'Don't Ask Me,' someone asked 'What makes quicksands?' So the organiser had to show how quicksands develop, and went to all the expense of coming over from the east coast by helicopter, landing on the foreshore right in front of our house at Grange. They made two trips, and they couldn't have come at a better time, because the sands were very dangerous when they first arrived. They sent a young lass in her twenties, and I took her out on to the sands. The river had just moved out and we had to keep going — the only thing to do if you walk out onto soft sand of this type. If a person is lightweight, and keeps moving he can get over it, whereas a horse would go down in it. The sand moved like jelly as I walked over with the young woman, and I told her she would be safe if she kept going. She was a bit hesitant about it, but when she had got over, she said it would be ideal for the programme. The television people then worked out a timetable and wrote to tell me when they would be over. The bay alters so quickly that by then it had filled in a lot and the sand had gone harder, but it was still bad enough.

Anyway, they came and landed the pilot and a stunt man, and the latter came into the house to change into a full-length rubber suit ready for the job. They thought the quicksands in Morecambe Bay were like those you see on Western films, where you just sink in to your armpits, shouting 'HELP', and someone comes along and pulls you out. It isn't like that at all. I told the stuntman that if he went in that deep, we would never get him out. We should pull him to pieces, but we wouldn't be able to get him out. The quicksands here, once you get in, set like cement. So I said that if he went in up to his knees that would be quite far enough.

They decided to do a dummy run. I could see he was a bit nervous; in fact, he was very nervous. He asked what to do if he felt himself going down; I replied, 'When tha feels theself goin' in, sit on thi arse.' He did just this, and it took two of us to pull him out. Now they were going to make the real film. The stuntman set off as if he was going for a walk, and suddenly, in he went! The helicopter came over, dropped a rope down over him and tried to pull him out, but couldn't. So they dropped another fellow down to try to help him, but now they were both going down in the sand. For a time it seemed as if they were pulling the helicopter down too, because as I explained, the sand sets solid around anything that has broken the crust and gone down in it. After several tries, they eventually got both men free and winched them up into the helicpoter, and away they went, back to the east coast.

Later on I received another letter saying they would like to come again. It was a different producer who came the next time, with a different helicopter and pilot. The sands had filled in a little bit more by then, of course. They brought a wooden dummy with them this time; I expect the last do had given them a shock, when they found it was so difficult getting the men out. The dummy was far too big: they had made it about eight feet tall. If they had made it half that size, it would have looked quite realistic as we sunk it in the sands, but because it was so tall, we had to sink it very deep. It went in all right and then the helicopter came over and let the rope down, lassoed it, and tried to winch it up. It wouldn't move! They tried and tried, but at last they had to leave it fast in the quicksands, as the tide was coming in. That dummy was there for weeks, and people kept ringing me up, saying there was a man drowning in the bay. Some days there was nothing of it to be seen, because it was right down under the sand, but on another occasion, when the tide had scoured round it, it was waist high in the water. This was the day I had been waiting for. When the tide was out, I walked over with a saw and sawed the dummy off at the waist. The rest of it is still down under the sands, but at least the phone calls have stopped.

On 9 September 1974, I received a letter with a request for my services as guide, to accompany a man and his Chinese wheelbarrow or desert cart, on the walk from one side of the bay to the other, a distance of nine or ten miles, depending on which way the wind was blowing.

What sort of project could this be, I wondered? I was not left to wonder long. A further letter came with all the details of the desert cart. It was a lightweight construction with a wheel 5ft in diameter, and long, narrow boxes, one on either side of the wheel, to carry the load. The disposal of the load in this way put the weight on the cart, not on the driver. A sail was used to take advantage of any favourable wind, leaving only the guiding of the cart to the driver and enabling him to cover many more miles than would have been the case had he to push or pull the load on a conventional cart. The whole idea was to test the cart out in the stringent conditions of the bay before taking it out to the Sahara Desert for a further test, after which it was hoped to put the cart into production. It would be of great use to the people of this kind of area, who could not afford to use motorised transport or camels to move their wares.

The design was based on the Chinese sailing wheelbarrow. A barrow or cart such as this has been used for over two thousand years by people of the Orient to carry loads many times their own weight. The vehicle was to be manufactured by a well-known British firm, and the Morecambe Bay test was covered by a BBC 'Nationwide' helicopter.

Although things went fairly well out in the Bay, it was apparently a different matter when the cart reached the Sahara. The fluctuations in wind strength there were much greater: at times it was so strong that the wheelbarrow had to be held firmly against it, then suddenly it would drop and the barrow would be over on its side. The wheels too were found to be too narrow, and all in all the going was very hard. The journey of two thousand miles took three months. Eventually it was decided not to put the cart into production, but the prototype is preserved in store at the Science Museum, South Kensington.

This was one of the more unusual trips I made across the bay. Another was when the Roundhead Association asked for my help when they wished to cross the sands with their army. This was a most interesting and picturesque walk or march, as all the people were dressed in the appropriate costumes and kept in formation. On the far side of the bay the Cavaliers were waiting, also in full dress, hidden in the bushes, and as the Roundheads drew near a cannon was fired. This was a signal for a pitched battle to begin. It was a beautiful day, and the river was only about knee-deep as we crossed. The battle lasted for about half an hour — a much shorter affair than when the real Roundheads were about in this area so many years ago.

I find all the walks interesting, but these two stand out as the most unusual, up to the present day. I was satisfied to think that I had brought several hundred more people safely over the treacherous sands by means of the knowledge I had gained in my day-to-day work.

In the last week of October 1975, I was approached by Granada Television to make a film which they called 'Sand Pilot'. The film ran for thirty minutes, and was shown at ten-thirty on the evening of 30 November. It was repeated the following summer on 'Granada Reports', after the news at six.

This was a film of the life of my family, showing how my work as a fisherman, fishing in some unusual ways, affects all of us. The family was seen helping with the cleaning and packing of the whitebait. This job has to be done whenever the whitebait come in from the nets; I have to fish the nets according to the tides, and whatever the time, we all have to get stuck in, working on until the last packet of fish is in the freezer. Since the whitebait, the very young herring, come in the colder weather, sorting them is a very cold and uncomfortable job.

But we are a very happy family and would not change our way of life; we have learned to take the bad times along with the good. Guide's Farm, sixteen years after we first came here, is now a very cosy home. Bill, Robert and Diane have homes of their own, and Olive and I have three lovely grandchildren. Paul, who was just a baby when I first met Olive, is working, while Jean is a teenager with a keen interest in the ponies we keep.

We are all agreed that, in spite of difficulties and hard work, life at Guide's Farm has, over the years, proved interesting and rewarding.

7 Crossing the Bay on Foot

From the moment of my appointment I was looking forward to my new post as guide, and I was not short of enquiries about the cross-bay walks, even during my first winter. Although the walking season does not start until the warmer weather comes along to cheer us up and the temperature of the water has risen several degrees, so that the walk can be an enjoyable experience rather than a cold and miserable one, there are many groups of people who want to plan a walk across Morecambe Bay as early in the year as possible.

I started off as I meant to go on. I chose the dates carefully and accurately in January, and these dates were then given to the Tourist Information Office and the local newspaper. Nowadays, with motorways making it so much easier to get to the Lake District and the Morecambe Bay area, the bay walks have become so popular that there is no need to advertise. The main worry is to keep the walks down to manageable proportions. Numbers have to be restricted to around 150, for safety reasons, and this number I find reasonably easy to control. On occasions I have found many more people waiting on the shore than I had booked, and if there were a few youngsters, and sometimes even older people, who did not take kindly to the discipline very necessary on a Morecambe Bay walk, it can take the pleasure out of the adventure for the others. I like the walks to be enjoyable for everyone, old and young.

Early in the New Year, letters start coming in, and the telephone is really a hot line — it never stops ringing, with enquiries from groups, clubs and individuals. All are welcome, but we must be well organised for walks of three and a half to four hours. I always try to please, but there is a limit to what one person can do, however dedicated to his job he may be, and in some circumstances a line has to be drawn.

Officially, my duties are set out as follows:

GUIDES OVER KENT AND LEVEN SANDS CHARITY.

NOTICE is hereby given by Order of the Chancellor of the Duchy of Lancaster and the Trustees of the above Charity that the Guide-over-Sands is authorised, instructed, and empowered as follows :-

1. That on no account is he to accept the conduct of any party of persons across the Sands (whatever the age of the persons) which exceeds in number 150.

2. That he shall not accept the conduct of the said maximum number of 150 persons or any less number out of a party of more than 150 requesting conduct if it be proposed that an excess over the maximum of 150 should follow behind as an "unofficial" party.

3. That if adverse conditions of weather, tide, visibility or otherwise are present, or, in the opinion of the Guide, might be likely to occur and render the crossing more than normally dangerous or hazardous, or which might make it impossible or doubtful to give proper conduct, and having also regard to the ages, conditions, or proposed mode of travel of the party or persons desiring to cross the Sands, he may at his discretion (and without giving his reasons) refuse to conduct any party, person or persons at all or only such number as in his sole discretion he considers wise or prudent (if at all) in the circumstances.

4. Any person or body of persons crossing or attempting to cross the Sands contrary to the above or after refusal by the Guide to conduct having regard to the foregoing, or who, during a crossing conducted by the Guide, fails to conform to any order, behest, instruction or request by the Guide in his official capacity concerning the crossing or the ordering thereof, does so at his, her, or their own risk. No responsibility is accepted by the Guide, the Trustees, or the Chancellor of the Duchy of Lancaster in respect of any accident to persons crossing the Sands even though under conduct of the Guide.

5. Organizers of parties desiring the services of the Guide for crossing the Sands for pleasure shall give adequate notice thereof to the Guide to enable him to make proper arrangements and fix times therefor and the Guide's decision as to date and time of crossing shall be final and must be adhered to.

E. G. Hargreaves

Clerk to the Trustees.

Dated 17th September 1964.

> The Guide shall be and shall continue to keep himself conversant with the tides, state and direction of channels, fords, quicksands and other similar matters bearing upon or affecting the safety of persons crossing the sands and all the best routes from time to time thereover, and in particular shall inspect and test the fording places each day and of such matters he shall render a half yearly report to the trustees on the thirtieth day of June and the thirty first day of December in every year.
>
> He shall also keep accurate record of all foot and horse, passengers and vehicles or by boat crossing the sands in each half year and his said report to the trustees shall embark details of such passengers for the same period.

But the guide's responsibilities have, of course, increased over the years as more and more people cross the sands. Usually he has no difficulty in accepting anyone who applies to him to take part in one or more of these organised walks, but he would certainly have the power to say no to anyone who he thought might cause trouble.

Seasons vary considerably, and so do the tides, the sands and the rivers. The stranger, who walks across one year and enjoys it, wonders why he cannot come on the walk on the same date the next year. He doesn't understand about the tides and how they alter, from high one week to low the next. Extremely high tides make the bay unsuitable for walking across. The rivers are swollen and there is no dry sand at all. Low tides make ideal conditions, if the weather is warm and sunny: for most of the walk, on the higher ground, the sand is firm and dry, reflecting the warmth of the sun and making it most enjoyable. About halfway across, after walking for an hour and a half, everybody is ready for a break, and the sand is dry enough to squat down on. I can tell that people are really enjoying this, as I watch them taking out their sandwiches and flasks of tea. I hear their conversations about the walk, perhaps comparing it with a previous walk they have taken part in. Most of them say they wouldn't have missed it for the world.

In some years, I can arrange many more walks than in other years. It all depends on the times of high water. I like to start off from the Morecambe side of the bay, as this is the most popular. I arrange for my party to be at the starting point at four hours ebb, which is four hours after high water. Allowances have to be made for people coming from all parts of the country. I do take some people on the shorter walk from Grange-over-Sands to Arnside, but the walk from Hest Bank is more popular, and I like to plan for an afternoon crossing. This gives people time to get to the starting point after lunch, and we can then reach Grange around teatime. All this has to be worked out with the aid of a time table. It is no use starting off too late or it would be well into the evening before the party reached Grange. There is also transport to be thought of, so that people on the walk can get home. So I plan everything to be convenient for everyone as far as I can, but the tide and the weather always have the last word.

Although the organising of the dates and times of the walks takes place as early as January, I cannot say at such an early stage just where will be the most suitable place to bring the parties in. The rivers, dykes and sand will be changing from day to day, tide to tide. I always keep an eye on these things and can usually foresee any changes which will be taking place, but then you get the extra high winds and the unpredictable tides, making changes which normally would not have occurred, while heavy rain can swell the rivers and help change the course.

As I go out on to the sands about my daily work — nightly, too, very often — I never let much happen without taking notice. I will have about four months now before the start of the walking season. This doesn't mean that I can forget about it all and just carry on with fishing. Each and every day, each tide, I look at the movement of the rivers, dykes and gullies. Many a time, I have it all worked out, right up to the last week or so before the start of the walks: where I would choose to cross the rivers; the most suitable place to come ashore with the party; the safest, firmest route across the sands . . . Then comes a sou'westerly gale, with the extra high tide; one or two days of solid rain, and the plans I have made all have to be scrapped. This is our bay, forever changing. This is what makes it so dangerous and yet so appealing.

Now the time for the first walk of the season draws nearer. It is to be a Sunday in May, starting from Morecambe Lodge, near Hest Bank. I have already had written confirmation, or a telephone message, giving me details of all who are to join the walk on this date. Keeping a watchful eye on those treacherous gullies, dykes and the ever-changing River Kent, I now have to make the crossing on foot, over the route I shall be following with the organised party the next day. Having to start from the opposite side of the bay from where I live is the first problem. I have to enquire about train times from Grange-over-Sands to Carnforth, and then I must make sure of getting a bus from there to Bolton-le-Sands, a small village on the outskirts of Morecambe. I walk the last mile from the bus to the shore. As I make my way down the winding road I see no one with whom to pass the time of day. A few more minutes now, and I shall be on the foreshore. This journey time has to be carefully calculated so that I start off on my journey across the sands four hours after high water, as I will be doing on the following day and must for the rest of the season.

With a slight westerly breeze blowing, visibility is very good. Looking to the south-west, I can get a grand view of Morecambe which brings back memories of earlier days, both of cockling on the sands and also of outings, as Morecambe is a good town for entertainment. In the far distance, to the west, I can see the huge cranes of the Barrow-in-Furness shipyard. Scanning the more northerly coastline, I can just make out the shape of the Hoad monument, which stands on the highest hill in Ulverston. It is said to be a copy of the Eddystone lighthouse, but gets the name 'pepperpot' from the local people.

Ulverston lies near to the estuary of the River Leven, which flows from Lake Windermere. The River Crake, coming from Coniston Water, also empties on to the sands between the Cartmel and Barrow-in-Furness peninsulas, making that area quite as dangerous as the rest of Morecambe Bay. Humphrey Head juts out into the sea, to the south of Kents Bank, with wooded slopes on its northern side. It was here, so history tells us, that the last wolf in England was caught by one of the knights of old.

Now, as I am about to start off on my exploratory walk, I can see Grange-over-Sands quite clearly, a compact little town on the hillside, with the differing shades of the trees, and the Lakeland hills in the background. Holme Island stands out just to the north of Grange, and from where I stand, Silverdale is hidden away round the corner of Jenny Brown's Point, while Arnside Knott rises up beyond.

A quick glance at my watch; shoes and socks off; trousers rolled up to the knees: I take my stick in my hand, throw my haversack over my shoulder, and make my way out into the bay. What a grand feeling this gives me! Fresh air and the smell of the sea breeze, and not a sight or sound of anyone except the squawk of the gulls in the distance. Whoops — nearly went down on my backside there! — it's a bit slippery near the edge of the marsh; I must watch out tomorrow, and warn the walkers. I wouldn't want any casualties at this stage of the walk, although it would be the best possible place if something really bad had to happen, rather than halfway across the bay, miles from anywhere.

I choose to walk due west at the start of the walk, just for half a mile or so, getting clear of the shore and making out into the bay, before turning gradually northward. Shortly, I can see what looks like a large mound of stone, with the odd very big boulder or two. One wonders what this mound can be doing, half a mile out from the shore. It is a 'skeer' or scar named Priest Scar, which probably, centuries ago, would have been linked up with the land.

Striding out now, at a good pace as the sand is very firm, I look towards Jenny Brown's Point, keeping a rough line as near as possible to that which I shall follow tomorrow with my walkers. Ahead of me now, but on a much lower level, I can see the River Keer. My eyes are everywhere. This river, smaller than the River Kent, can be very dangerous, and has to be forded. It is often shallow but it is noted for its quicksands, so I know I must be wary and find the most suitable and safe place to cross.

On the path I am taking, I can now see clearly, as I drop to the much lower level near the river, that I will have to make a detour of about four hundred yards to my right. Straight ahead is a sharp 'brack' where the bank of the river has broken away as the tide has scoured under it. This is another hazard to be faced when walking out in the bay. You can be standing on the bank of the river on seemingly solid sand, when suddenly a yard or two of the banking just topples into the water. The underwater current has been eating away at the sand and all at once there is no support for quite a large piece, and anyone standing on it will be thrown into the fast-flowing river. It can be like dropping off a cliff. I've seen some of these bracks or breakaways fifteen feet deep; if they are close in to the shore, markers are often put in to warn bathers when the tide covers these very dangerous areas.

All this I am looking at as I make my way over the ground where I shall be leading my party tomorrow. I need to find a place where I can spread the people out. There will be about 150 walkers, so I'm looking for a long stretch of level sand; I don't want everyone to have to cross the river in one spot, where the bed may be soft. These are my thoughts as I walk down into the bed of the River Keer. I find it reasonably firm at the start, then the odd few yards move like jelly under my feet and I quicken my pace. You keep moving on sand like this. The river is fairly shallow at this time, but the sand underneath is bad, really frightening in some places. I stride quickly out on to higher, firmer ground on the other side; looking back, I study new ground a few yards to either side of my crossing place. Now I have to think about tomorrow.

Providing the weather stays fine, we shall make it across safely, but I must tell the party what to expect before we start; and instead of having them following in each other's footsteps, I will spread them out to the left and right of me. I must see that they keep to these instructions and ask them to walk steadily across, quickening pace as soon as they feel the sand starting to move under their feet. They must not stop. They must keep going, and make on to new ground if the sand is really soft.

This advice is usually appreciated by everyone, and if the party keeps to it we shall have no trouble. All this is going through my mind as I decide to make a re-check before setting out on my journey once more, and I store all these points in the back of my mind for tomorrow. The tides are low, and now as I walk on higher ground, away from the Keer, the sand is very firm and dry.

From now on, for the next hour or so, I shall not have much to worry about. As I approach a small dyke, I look to my left, which is due west, and see that the River Kent has moved considerably towards the Silverdale - Bolton-le-Sands side of the bay since my crossings last season. This means that I shall have to keep a sharp eye on things and perhaps stay much nearer to the coast than we normally do on our walks. I go on now at a steady pace, looking well ahead, for sand-marks and landmarks all have to be remembered. By now, I am nearly halfway across, having kept a straight course for Jenny Brown's Point, after crossing the River Keer.

The land appears to be getting closer, and eventually I am walking parallel with the marsh. Rather than go up on to the marsh at this stage, I keep about a hundred yards away, as the sand is still firm. I know, though, that before I can stop for a break of ten to fifteen minutes, I have to make my way over a really nasty little gully. It comes out from the land, winding its way over the marshes and on into the River Kent. When the tides are low and the weather favourable, I know I can cross it with very little difficulty, but after a heavy night's rain it could set me a problem. All is well, though, and once again I take notice of the area I have crossed and feel satisfied that I can settle for this route tomorrow. I feel ready now for a break after walking for an hour and a half, so I look around for a dry patch to sit on and enjoy my orange and the tranquillity of my surroundings . . .

Time now to press on again, making my way right out into the bay, on nice firm sand; but after a mile or so the ground drops down a good ten feet to another dyke coming out from the land. I would expect problems here after heavy rain, but today it is safe and I cross it without difficulty; the bottom is a little soft, especially towards the far side, but there is nothing to worry about unduly. Now I am on firm sand again, but it is rough and rutted, and not so good on the feet!

I now make a change in direction. Seeing the River Kent in the distance, I line up the headland of Jenny Brown's Point and the bathing pool at Grange-over-Sands, and follow on that line, watching the shallow dykes and gullies. The ripples on the sand made by the ebb tide tell me how fast the tide moves in that area. As I approach the river, I can see clearly where to make my crossing. Although, at this point, the river is very wide, the bed is reasonably flat, both entering the water and coming out at the other side. My judgement tells me the water should be about knee-deep at this time. With the dry summer, little or no fresh water is coming down from the hills surrounding the bay, so the current is not too swift.

Wading warily and steadily, I use my stick to find out whether any object has been left by the ebb tide along my path, causing the flowing river to scour round it and make a deep hole. Even an old tree trunk, the wood sodden with the salt water and too heavy to float, can be brought down the river and left like this. I never take chances when fording the rivers, since it is easy to drop down out of your depth; the cold water gives you a great shock when you are not expecting a ducking, especially if you are not so young. So I never go blithely on, but prod the ground with my long staff as I cross these areas.

Now, with the river safely crossed, and feeling well satisfied with conditions, I continue my journey towards Grange-over-Sands. At a rough guess, I should reach Grange, at this pace, within the hour. Sometimes the land seems to recede instead of coming closer; this is caused by tricks of the light and the atmosphere. But I know that I have made good time, and that it won't be long before I am crossing the last stretch of water, near to the shore at Grange, and walking up on to the promenade.

At last I reach the rocks on Grange shore, and sit down for a few minutes' well-earned rest. I then wash my feet, if I can find a puddle, and let the breeze dry them. Next, on with my socks and shoes, which I have carried over in my haversack. Looking back across the sands, I am pleased with myself and feel that I have taken a lot of worry off my shoulders for the walk tomorrow.

The journey over the bay has taken me three and a half hours. Now, a ten-minute walk should get me home, where my wife will be expecting me. She will have been able to keep an eye on me out there, from our bedroom window, as I have a very powerful telescope, essential for the work I have to do out in the bay. It is an ex-naval prismatic monocular gun-sighting telescope, made of brass and weighing 15½lb. I always tell Olive, before setting out, the approximate times at which I shall be in certain places, so she knows in which direction to look. One thing I am certain of — a good meal will be waiting for me!

After the meal, I feel ready for some relaxation, and a good night's sleep, before the big event tomorrow.

On Sunday morning I am up bright and early. The walk is due to start at twelve noon, so I have plenty of time to do a few jobs around the house. The telephone keeps ringing: people are asking if the walk is still on, as it is not the best of days, with a slight, fine drizzle making visibility rather poor. 'Yes' is my answer to all the callers. Whatever rain comes now cannot make much difference to our walk. The chief hazard is constant, heavy rain on the previous day, which, after soaking the land, floods into the rivers. But no, not today: the going is pretty good, I tell them.

I am lucky on this occasion to have been offered a lift to the other side of the bay by car. A family from the next village wanted to join the walk; their father offered to take them, and also to give me the opportunity of travelling with them. As I wait for the family to arrive, I make sure that I have my whistle and my stick, as these are the things by which I am recognised when I reach the foreshore ready to start the walk. 'Here he is,' says one chap as soon as I reach the party. 'That's him,' says another; 'I've seen 'im on the telly.'

I make my way over to have a word with their leaders, who usually come forward and introduce themselves, telling me about the people in their parties and where they are from. I am amazed at times when I hear how far some of them have travelled to do the walk.

As the time for the start draws near, I whistle them all up together. I must ask them all to make it an enjoyable walk and not to hurry the pace, as I shall have to stop more often to let the stragglers catch up if we walk too quickly. I also ask them to keep behind the guide at all times. They must never get in front, as there are some places where I know the sand is a bit soft, and when we reach these areas I shall blow my whistle to get their attention. Finally, I want them all to enjoy themselves. Now, up and away we go.

It is not a fine day like yesterday, as we make our way off the marsh and down on to the sand. I remember about slipping, so I shout to the walkers to tread carefully until we get clear of the mud and well out into the bay. There is no sight of Grange today — just a grey mist ahead. I must remember the dykes and gullies from yesterday. I know just where I am, as I reach the sand and landmarks I stored in my memory for this walk. Although visibility is poor, we shall reach the other side in safety.

The start of the walk is often very much like the start of a race. Some walkers make up to the front of the group and keep that position all the way across. I get questions fired at me from left, right and centre. It is always the same question from youngsters; 'How far to the river, mister?' As we splash and splosh, I think to myself of yesterday, and the peace and quiet. Today is so different, but no less interesting to me.

A group of strong lads kick a ball around to my left. As long as they stay to the left I am quite happy. 'I'm going to stay near the guide,' I hear one ten-year-old saying. What an adventure this is for these town lads. I try to recall what I thought about it all when I was their age, but then, I was taken out on to the bay as soon as I could walk. Another lad asks me how I know the way, and 'How long will it be before the tide comes in, mister?' 'How deep is the river?' 'Can we swim in it?' And so it goes on, question after question, for most of the journey. I answer them patiently, but now I must concentrate, as we approach the River Keer. I stop the party well away from the river, waiting for those at the rear to catch up; when they are all together, I blow my whistle to attract their attention, and tell them what I would like them to do. Getting them in order is quite easy: now for the OFF.

Yesterday, the river bed had to take my weight only. Today is quite different, with the weight of 150 people, some sticking too close together for safety, which makes matters worse. The sand has softened up pretty badly in places, but in spite of a few shrieks and screams, I haven't lost anyone! I like the walkers to see a bit of this sort of sand, from time to time, so that they realise what dangers can be encountered on walks across a bay like this. A person may come on the walk one year and cross quite easily, without getting into such an area as we have just come through. He then gets the idea that it is plain sailing, and may be tempted to go out on his own. So I think it is good for all of them to see the dangers. It is never straightforward.

Without the knowledge that I have gained during the many years I have walked these sands, it is impossible to cross safely, and it should never be attempted.

Now the misty rain is cutting down visibility to about half a mile, so the walkers are beginning to understand the dangers and are sticking closely together. The games have stopped and the youngsters have quietened down.

Now I must take my bearings from the sand, so after coming out from the River Keer I take note of the ridges. All the smaller dykes I encountered yesterday were running east to west, so the ridges made on the sand by the tide as it went out should, by my calculations, be running north to south. As we are going to the north, we just keep going along the ridges. I have very few interruptions from the walkers now — all are watching the ridges in the sand! As I went over this area yesterday, I know that before long, Jenny Brown's Point will be looming up in front of us. Yes, there it is and in these conditions it seems suddenly to appear from nowhere. 'How far have we gone now, mister?' 'Are we nearly there?' the younger ones ask. 'Almost halfway,' I tell them. Some of these young ones got such a soaking way back at the River Keer that now they are beginning to tire. Their jeans are sodden and are no doubt rubbing and chafing their legs. A good tip for the future, you young ones, keep as dry as you can, at least until you get to the main river, the Kent. You'll learn. Next walk you come on, you won't lark about in the first drop of water you get to!

We now approach the last gully before we go up on to the marsh for a break, and looking to see the best spot to cross, I notice something lying in a scoured-out place a few yards away. I walk over and find it is a sheep embedded in the sand. 'Can I have a few of you strong men over here, please?' Several come running. We start to scoop the sand from around the animal with our hands, and after some hard work think we have shifted enough to be able to pull him out. But even though only a few inches of his feet are still in the sand, we cannot move him and have to dig until we have him out completely. We carry him up well above the tideline and leave him where he can get some grass, if he is able to feed. We shall have to phone the farmer as soon as we reach Grange.

All the party get through in fine style and now we need to find a good place to rest our legs. Blowing the whistle, I shout, 'Stopping here for a break of fifteen to twenty minutes.' Everyone finds a dry place to sit down, and out come the lunch boxes. We are glad of this little rest. Ridged sand is not easy to walk on, especially with bare feet. I don't get much of a break. Someone is sure to come over to ask questions, but I oblige and tell them what I can. The time has flown answering all these questions; I look at my watch and blow my whistle to get the party on the move once more.

Half an hour's walking from here should bring us to the River Kent. This is what the younger ones have been waiting for. Now that the river is in sight, I know that it is quite safe for them to stay awhile, splashing one another and in some cases even swimming fully clothed! The fun these youngsters get out of this is really good to see. After they have had their fling, I look again at my watch and say to myself, 'Time to move on, Ced, whistle 'em up!' They all make out to the side, some very reluctant to leave the water. Now I have the party all together again, we make off in a line for Grange-over-Sands.

I take the pace a bit slower now, as some of the younger ones are wet through. As it has been a day of misty rain, most have kept their jeans on for warmth, but now they are finding their wet clothes a bit uncomfortable. At the rear, I can see one or two with their legs wide apart, so they must be chafed: these few, I bet, are wishing it was over. Grange bathing pool appears out of the mist, and the pace begins to quicken. Looking over my shoulder, I can see a few at the rear, having a job to keep up with the rest, so a word is needed from me to slow the party down, otherwise we shall have to stop. This, I find is a regular thing. Whereas I know that there is still quite a way to go, some of the walkers do not realise the distance we have still to cover and start pushing the pace to the limit. I'm a very patient man, but now they are beginning to try me. 'STOP' Blowing my whistle as loudly as I can, I address them firmly. 'You are not home and dry yet, so please slow the pace down to suit the others.' That seems to have sunk in, and we move on at a more reasonable speed, as a party of walkers should. But not for long. 'Can we be the first on to the shore, sir?' a young 'un

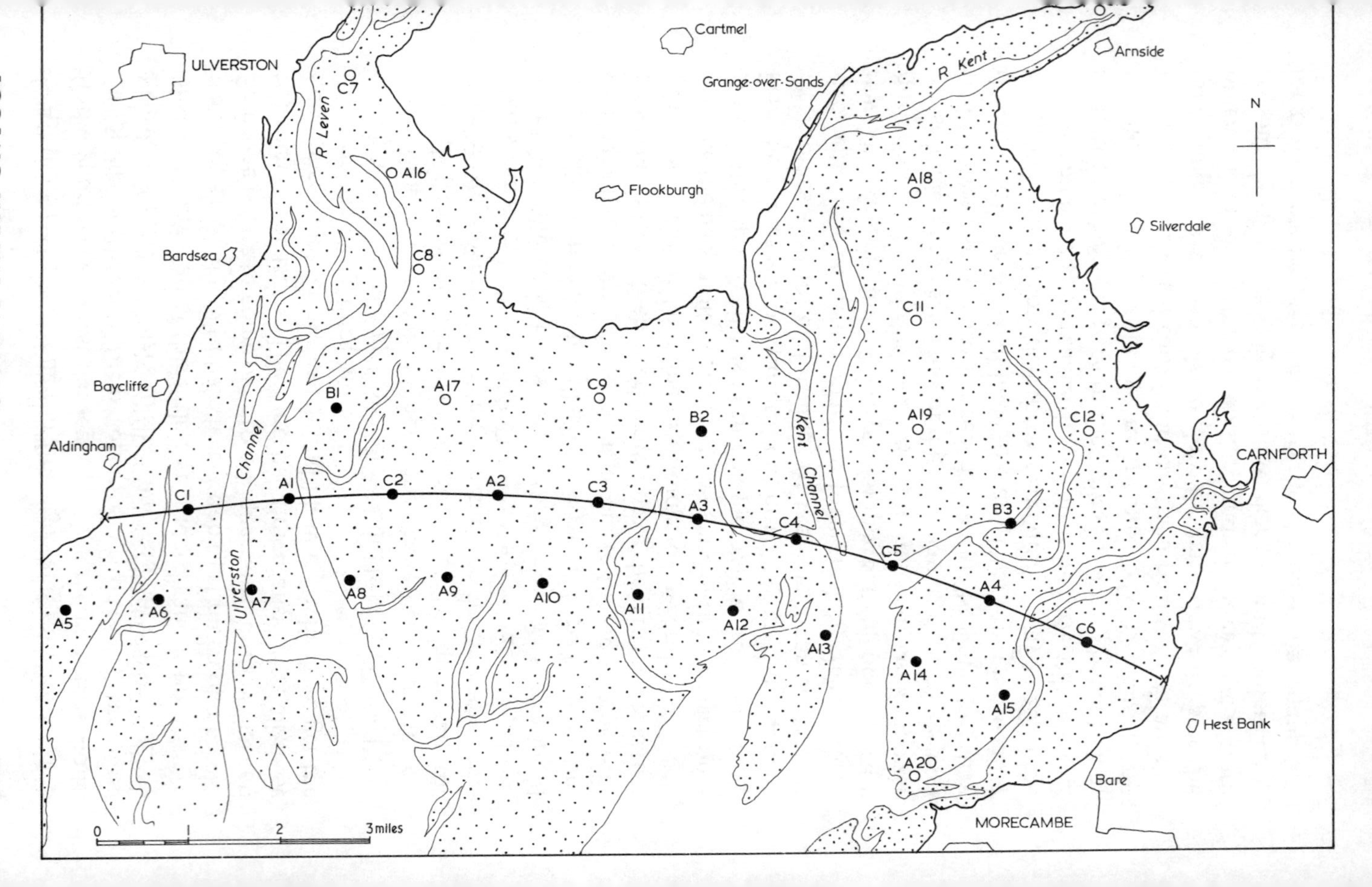
ULVERSTON
Cartmel
Arnside
R Leven
Grange-over-Sands
R Kent
N
Flookburgh
Silverdale
Bardsea
Baycliffe
Aldingham
Channel
Ulverston
Kent Channel
CARNFORTH
Hest Bank
Bare
MORECAMBE
0
1
2
3 miles
C7
A16
C8
A18
C11
A17
C9
B1
B2
A19
C12
C1
A1
C2
A2
C3
A3
C4
C5
A4
C6
B3
A5
A6
A7
A8
A9
A10
A11
A12
A13
A14
A15
A20

shouts. 'Aw reet, but wait till we get to the last hundred yards or so.'

Nearing Grange, I can see crowds of people waiting for the walkers. Visitors to the area probably have never seen anything like this before, and are quite taken with such a sight. All is well now, and to those who have been eagerly awaiting my word I shout, 'Get ready, GO!' About fifteen or twenty youngsters dash off, each trying to beat the rest to the shore. Now I can relax, just telling them to make over to the left of the bathing pool. I direct the walkers over the last hundrd yards, and when the last one is ashore I make my way up to the rocks and look back over the sands, the way we have come. Most of the party say as they pass how much they have enjoyed the walk, and thank me for leading them safely across. I get many enquiries both from onlookers and from those who have taken part in the crossing. 'When is the next walk across the sands?' 'May we come again?' 'I'd love to,' another chips in. 'How often can this be done?' someone asks. 'Can anybody join in the walk?' One question after the other is answered, then walkers begin to make their way towards the promenade and their waiting transport takes them back home.

Now the shore is quiet again. I put my socks and shoes on and make my way home, ready for a meal and a well-earned rest. I am pleased with the walk, for crossing the sands in safety is a satisfying achievment.

In this era of high-speed trains and motorways, the walk has become a feat to be undertaken for the pleasure of being able to say, 'I have walked across the sands of Morecambe Bay.' Those who come over with the official guide can have a certificate to prove it!

The Morecambe Bay barrage survey. The black circles denote boreholes in part one of the survey, the white circles those in part two; the line between the two crosses shows the probable line of the proposed barrage. This map dates from April 1967; comparison with the map on pp 00-00 will show the considerable alteration in the channels between 1967 and 1979.

8 Foolhardy Walkers and Riders

In many of the parish churches around the wide area of Morecambe Bay, there are records of lives lost during the crossing of the sands. One of the most poignant is a gravestone in Cartmel Priory which tells of a mother and her son of twenty-six years. The son was drowned while trying to cross the bay, and his mother died almost a year later at nearly the same spot. This kind of tragedy was an all too common occurrence in the days before the coming of the Furness Railway.

Those making the hazardous journey on foot were not the only ones at risk. There was a regular coach service from Hest Bank to Kents Bank, and from there on to Ulverston. The coaches and wagons, drawn by horses, made the journey if tide and weather permitted; but the weather could change so quickly, and the quicksands alter so much, that the traveller was taking his life into his hands. There were times when one wheel of a cart went down into a hole, throwing all the passengers into the water, and many were drowned in this way in the early 1800s.

On one occasion a party was coming home from Ulverston fair, late on an October evening, when the cart overturned in the notorious hole named Black Scar. There were nine people on the cart, and amongst them a young couple who were to be married the next day. All were drowned, and all were buried in the churchyard of Cartmel Priory. The cart was later brought ashore and sold. Some years afterwards, twelve young men borrowed the same cart to drive across the bay to the fair at Lancaster. Black Scar again took its toll and all twelve were drowned.

With such a history, it is not surprising that the bay should have a reputation as a dangerous place to cross. In my capacity as guide I am always being consulted about the sands, and though I am not 'on duty' all the time, I am out there so much in the course of my work that little happens without my knowledge. Nowadays, when someone is in difficulties I will usually be around to help, and as a member of the auxiliary coastguard I have more than once assisted in a rescue. But I do not have responsibility for those who go out against my advice, or perhaps without consulting me.

Is it difficult to cross Morecambe Bay, either by the long route, Hest Bank to Grange-over-Sands, or by the short route, Grange-over-Sands to Arnside? Physically it is not; but it would be extremely dangerous and foolish even to think of leaving the shore at either side of the bay without the company of a guide, or without at least making a visit or phone call to the guide's home beforehand to find out the time and state of the tides. It is too late when you find yourself out in the middle of the bay, and suddenly the tide appears as if from nowhere, cutting you off from the land.

The tide comes up the rivers in a wave or bore, at a terrific speed; it can be as much as three feet high in certain conditions, though this varies considerably according to the expanse of the river bed. When the sand has been left fairly flat, it spreads over a large area and is like a low wall of water coming at you relentlessly. You could never outrun it. On the highest tides, or 'top of the flood' as we fishermen say, the tide travels as fast as a good horse. Even so, a good horse will tire eventually. Not so the tide. It waits for no one, and gathers speed as it builds up in the estuaries and dykes. With a strong tide running, the whole bay can be flooded in half an hour or less.

I have been out on a number of occasions to help people in difficulties. I well remember one incident which occurred soon after I took up the job of guide. I had just come back from shrimping with my son Bill. We were getting ready to boil the shrimps when, glancing out of the window, I saw two young girls making their way out into the bay. We dropped everything and raced over the railway line, which runs directly in front of Guide's Farm, acting as an embankment to keep the tide at bay. Slithering down the rocks on the other side, we both ran as fast as we could from the shore and out on to the sand. The girls were too far out to have heard our shouts, but I knew they were near to the river, and that shortly we too would be at risk from the tide. I made a quick decision. 'Bill,' I shouted, 'I'll take my thigh boots off and run like hell. Thee make back to shore. Keep an eye on us through t'glass.' He dashed away, but before he was out of earshot I shouted again. 'If it's too late to get back this side' — I gulped for breath; running so fast and so far I could hardly speak — 'I'll . . . make . . . for . . . Arnside.' That would be the safest thing to do as I could see higher ground over the river which would not be covered until later. I knew exactly where and when the tide would be at any point in the river, and if I couldn't make the girls hear me it would certainly be too late to get back to Grange. We should have to cross the river.

The girls were plodding on and I tried shouting to them again, but the wind, which gets stronger when the tide comes in, carried my voice away and I thought I would never make them hear me. I raced on; suddenly, one of them looked round. I stopped to get my wind, and waved my arms, beckoning them to come back to me. I was thankful that at last I had managed to get their attention and that I hadn't to run any farther out, knowing that every minute the tide was getting nearer and would soon cut off our chance of reaching the shore. I waved frantically, and they started to run towards me; I had one eye on my watch and the other on the tide. As they reached me, I told them we should have to run as fast as we could, and even then we would be lucky if we reached the shore. They looked at me as if I was speaking double Dutch, and I thought, 'Ced, lad, you can pick 'em.' Neither of them could speak a word of English! So I turned them to face the shore and beckoned them to follow me, pointing to the oncoming tide. A look of horror came on their faces and they started to run. We had just made the safety of the rocks near the bathing pool when the tidal bore passed, raging along the rocks like nothing, I am certain, that these two girls had ever seen before.

Whether they thanked me or not, I will never know. Their language was beyond me. There was some slight consolation, however. A bystander who had seen the near-tragedy rang the local newspaper, and the next evening there were a couple of paragraphs about how the Grange guide and his son had risked their lives by running out on to the sands in the face of the oncoming tide to save two young girls, bringing them back safely to the shore. That was the only 'near do' that summer, though there were more to follow.

Gaining access to the shore at Grange-over-Sands is quite different from the easy approach at Flookburgh where all my young days were spent. There, a straight road, a good mile long, leads to quite a big stretch of marsh, an ever-open gateway to the sea. When fishing and following the tides, we were coming and going at all times of the day and night. Now, in my new job as guide at Grange, I had the inconvenience of having to cross the railway line. I was lucky to have a level crossing as near as a hundred yards away, but I had to have the permission of the crossing keeper before going over. There might be quite a long wait if a train was due, and this didn't go down so well, especially in the middle of a wet night. Sometimes when a relief man was on duty I would think that I could have been to my nets and back before the train he was waiting for reached the crossing; but he knew the rules, and I knew he wouldn't let me through until the train had passed, so I just had to wait until he gave me the 'all clear'.

In an emergency, such a hold-up would be even more serious, because you cannot afford to waste time before getting out on to the sands. One day, a man I knew, came rushing up to me, binoculars in hand, shouting 'Ced, Ced, get tractor out, I've seen a couple of silly beggars way out on yon banking. We'll just make it if tha hurries.' I started up the tractor and just got to the crossing as the gates were being opened. What a bit of luck! Down the causeway, across the short stretch of sand, and there in front of us was the river to ford. It was about knee-deep and we were soon on the other side.

I shouted 'Hold on!' as I throttled back on the old Fordson Major, and away we went. These two people were like dots on the horizon. 'Risking our necks out here again' was the thought that ran through my mind, and I was worried too about the old tractor. If it decided to stop out here, we would all be gonners: this never enters your head when you go out on the sands at the right time. We'd soon be on our way back to safer places, I was thinking, when my mate said to me sheepishly, 'Lookster theer, Ced, yon beggars are safer than me and thee.' The two young people were sitting in a very shallow small boat! We turned tail as fast as we could and were glad to hear the rattle of the loose shale and shingle under our wheels as we made our way up on to the shore. We really had been caught out that time; we were so disgusted when we saw they were in a boat that we never uttered a word. I didn't put much faith in my friend's binoculars after that: and if I had had time to look through my own, that wasted journey would have been avoided.

When a couple of bright young lads wanted to start pony treks across the sands of Morecambe Bay, I could foresee endless difficulties for such an undertaking. I explained the sort of trouble they could find themselves in with even half a dozen inexperienced riders: however good a rider may be on a field and fell, it is quite a different matter going through dykes, where the bottom may be soft, and fording the rivers, with a pony not used to this sort of thing. I told them I would not advise it under any circumstances, but they would not take no for an answer.

Sure enough, the following weekend, when I was bringing a party of over a hundred people across the bay, there were ten riders on their ponies waiting for us to move off. Once again, I told them I would not be held responsible, as it was against my advice that they were making the trek. Undeterred, they said they would follow me, and the leader added with a shrewd grin, 'You're not going to lead your party into the quicksands, so we shall be OK.'

We moved off with the ponies following in the rear, and the walk went off without much incident until, getting within sight of Grange-over-Sands, the leader of the riders thought he was home and dry and went on ahead. Knowing he was heading for a danger spot, I blew my whistle, but, though he turned to look, he waved his intention of making for the shore. The next thing we saw was the first rider, the leader himself, flying through the air and landing in some shallow water. His pony had gone into some soft sand. As the second rider was hard on the heels of the first, the same thing happened to him. The other riders stopped and waited for us to get within hailing distance, and I told them which course to take to avoid any further trouble. Meanwhile, the two ponies had managed to free themselves after a struggle and their very wet riders had remounted. When my party of walkers reached the shore there was no sign of the riders at all.

Needless to say, on the next walk there were no ponies and riders tagging on, so we were able to enjoy ourselves as usual. It had spoilt the previous walk, having ponies continually pushing you on. Though I had told the men that neither I nor the trustees would be reponsible for them or their party, they were still foolhardy enough to make the attempt. However, there has been no more talk of pony trekking across the sands to this day, and I hope there never will be.

Anyone who lives by the sea has always at the back of his mind the thought that there may be a tragedy. With quicksands close in to the shore, holidaymakers and sea anglers are the people mostly at risk. They come from the towns, often with very little idea of the dangers of estuaries. Morecambe Bay has many areas of shifting sands and a great deal of ingenuity has gone into the latest aids toward effecting the rescue of someone trapped in the awful clutch of the unyielding quicksand.

The mud-sledge, a flat-bottomed, fibreglass 'tray' measuring about 5ft by 3ft is brought as near as possible to the victim along with a thin wooden platform, made of slats to prevent too much suction. A line fired from the shore is attached by a wire rope to the front of the sledge, which is pulled alongside the trapped person. The two men in the sledge place the wooden platform over the person to be rescued; this enables the two rescuers to stand one on each side if need be, or they can work from the sledge itself. They have to work quickly if the tide is due. They carry in the sledge a suction pump with which they can direct a strong jet of water through a long nozzle down towards the feet of the victim, to liquefy the sand and enable him to be eased out of what might have been his grave.

The fire brigade can help with their equipment, with a powerful water jet, if the distance from the shore is not too great. But the best thing is to keep out of dangerous areas. To be rescued, you have first to be seen to be in danger, and in the vast expanse of an estuary *you may not be seen.* The mud-sledge is a life-saver where the foreshore is the scene of the accident, but out in the middle of the bay where the real quicksands are, only the presence of a fully experienced, authorised guide can lead people away from the danger that may be encountered.

On one occasion a foreign firm came over with a small-wheeled tractor-type vehicle which they said could do anything. They wanted it taken out into quicksands, and for it to be well and truly stuck. Since they wanted it in a really bad area, I brought it up from the other side of Humphrey Head, right near to Cart Lane crossing where there is a freshwater spring coming into the bay. I had left my own tractor with its engine running nearby. Well, I stood there and watched this marvel settle right up to its chassis. Then we tried to drive it out, but it couldn't get out under its own power. It had a winch on it, so we ran a long wire from the vehicle to a tree on shore — and pulled the front of it right off! Because of the suction of the sand, you can't pull anything straight out like that. A wing was pulled off and ripped to pieces in the effort to get it out. It ended up with me having to get the rest of it out with my old tractor.

That was the end of that miracle, which was supposed to be the vehicle that could do the almost impossible. If only they had known something about quicksands before they had designed it! The wheels were too small for a start. With the vibration of its engine, the wheels went into the sand right away, and once the wheels were under the sand, the tractor was powerless. The sand held it so fast that it might just as well have been set in cement. Our tractors have the biggest wheels possible with a wide tread to the tyres, so that we can go over soft sand and also keep well above any shallow water we may have to go through. The thing is to keep moving on quicksands, if you are unlucky enough to find any.

I have said before, and I will stress again, that there is no route or path which can be taken regularly, in safety, over the sands of Morecambe Bay. In November 1963, sixteen Royal Marines on a route march from Hest Bank to Barrow-in-Furness nearly got themselves into serious trouble before I rushed out and put them back on to a safe course. They had started out one hour before I had suggested, and so were heading straight for deep water. Then there was a lad who tried to cross the bay on a bicycle, but soon found out how hopeless it was when he had to be rescued in mid-channel. Changes are so diverse and so frequent. Each tide shifts the sand in one direction or another, and along the coast, quite large chunks of rock can be moved great distances. Even to someone with experience, such conditions are not always easily predicted.

I found it difficult to explain these possible hazards over the telephone to someone who had already made up his mind to bring a group of people over the sands on a certain date. I was not contacted until the last minute, before they started off, when conditions were found to be really bad. Having given them the fullest instructions possible, I was asked if I would walk out and ford the river to meet the party. As it turned out, I was very glad that I did go out on this occasion.

Crossing the river was difficult, although I had crossed it many times during the summer at almost the same point with quite large parties. It was very different this time, as heavy rain had fallen in the last few days and the river was in a dangerous state. Normally the water would be just knee-deep, but I could tell that I should be lucky if I made it through to the other side. I always carry a stout stick, and now I was very glad of it as I made my way into the fast-flowing river. I seemed to be making very little headway as I fixed my eyes firmly on the sandbank across the water, taking short steps and keeping my feet on the bottom as much as possible, just sliding them forward slowly. I knew that if I lifted them as I normally would, I would lose my balance, and I couldn't afford to get soaked with people depending on my getting through safely.

All sorts of things go on in your mind at a time like this, when so much fresh water is coming down the rivers to make them dangerous. I'm almost halfway through now, and I know I can make it if I can just keep my balance in the strong current, though the water is much deeper than I anticipated. With all the fresh water the sand had been scoured from the river bed, 'Too far now to turn back, Ced,' I say to myself, and I go on. Holding my pants and rolling them up as far as they will go doesn't stop them from getting wet. The rollers are like white horses creeping up to my waist now. Almost through to the other side, but the river doesn't get any shallower until the last few yards. It has taken quite a bit of strength out of me, and my main worry now is whether the party will have the courage to go back through the river with me under these conditions.

To make matters worse, the leader had taken them upriver from where I had come across and was leading them into what I knew was a very deep place with a lot of patches of soft sand. I had given them clear instructions at an earlier date, when conditions were favourable, but they were ignoring everything I had told them. My patience was beginning to wear thin, as the walk had taken place against my advice in the first place. Somehow, and before very long, I had to get some of the party to look my way, but no matter how much I waved my arms and my stick in the air, they took no notice at all. I suppose they were wondering what I was doing out there, and what I was getting so mad about.

Eventually I reached the tail end of the group, and told them I was the guide. 'Our guide's up at the front,' one of them said, looking at me as if to say, 'Go and get drowned.'

'In the first place, there is only one guide officially appointed for this side of the bay, and I am that guide,' I said. 'Now, as far as your guide goes, follow him if you like, but you will all have to turn round eventually when word gets through to those in front. No one but me can get you safely through that river and into Grange-over-Sands.' As I pointed to the river, swollen with the rains of the last few days, it looked almost impossible to cross. Three or four hundred yards wide, and swift-flowing like rapids, it was enough to scare the daylights out of most of them. I could read their thoughts as they looked towards the expanse of water. 'Yes, we have that to cross,' I said. I knew they were wondering who had brought them across the first stretch of sand and into the dangerous plight they were now in. I could see they were beginning to doubt the ability of their 'guide'.

Now, they decided they had better co-operate. A youngster in the group suggested that he should run on ahead and pass the word to all the others. As he neared the rest of the party, I could see they were stopping in their tracks. Word had passed along the line now, and we watched them hesitate; then I could see that my message had gone home, as they turned and made their way back along the route they had just taken. From the time I left home until I reached the far side if the river, where I expected to meet them, one and a half hours had passed. If things didn't get into some sort of order soon, it would be too late on the tide to attempt the rest of the journey.

At last they were all gathered round. Their leader was saying very little. I could see there was some unrest amongst the party, with some of them not wanting to go on. The walk was apparantly in the nature of a pilgrimage for this group of people, and there was a kind a desperation among them, a feeling that they must cross the bay at all costs. I calmed them down, congratulating them on the fact that, although they had made a bad start by getting two of their party stuck in the quicksands, they had managed to free them; though they were covered in sand and rather wet, they semed little worse for their ordeal. The party had however covered more miles than they would have done had they kept to the instructions their leader was given. He had not yet learned that the sands will always win if you don't respect them.

Now one of them spoke out for some of the senior citizens. 'I think it is asking too much for them to go on; some of them are already tired, and there is the river crossing ahead. That will be just impossible in their present state. Is there any chance of getting back to the shore?' she asked. I looked shorewards and could see that, with common sense, keeping well clear of the quicksands they had gone into on the way out, they could get ashore at Silverdale. There, they would have to arrange what transport they could to get back home. A quick decision was made on this and about a dozen or so decided to take this much easier way out.

The remainder were glad to let me organise those who had chosen to go on. I stressed at this point that this was an unofficial walk, taken against my considered judgement, and that neither the trustees nor I could be responsible for them in any way whatever; however, I would do my best to see that they all reached Grange safely. This agreed, we started off towards the river. There was nothing to fear, I assured them, so long as they listened to my instructions and did as I asked.

I chose the sturdy ones for the right flank and the tall ones to go in front. They must not look down at the moving water, or they would feel dizzy. The ones on the right were to take the main force of the water, and I went out in front with my staff to test the sand as far as I could. I fitted all the others in as tightly as sardines so that they could not see how bad conditions really were as we made our way slowly into the fast-running river. The water rose to our knees and then to our thighs. It took all my strength to hold my balance against it, out there in front, but we were coming into shallower water now. Behind us was a crossing that had seemed almost impossible. Only one rather elderly woman, who had not wished to return to the shore with the others, gave us some uneasy moments: two strong lads had to almost carry her through the worst part of the river. She was struck with nerves and her legs turned as if to jelly; prompt action had to be taken to get her through this frightening experience, the like of which she would never want to go through again. But as we made our way onwards and the coastline of Grange came into view, her strength returned and she went gamely on, the colour flooding into her cheeks again.

There was no quickening of pace with this party, as is usual when once the river is behind us. As we came within a couple of hundred yards of the shore, I pointed out the way for them to take, and waited until the last walker passed me. As each one went past, I had a few words with him. Usually, people wait until they get home from their holiday before they let me know how much they have enjoyed the walk across the bay, but these people made a point of telling me now. Though very wet, they were all thankful that I had gone out to help them to complete their journey in safety. I was only too pleased to see everyone safely across: had I not been there on this occasion, I hardly dare to think what would have happened. These people had really walked the bay, and would remember it for the rest of their lives.

9 Morecambe Bay Barrage Survey

The first news of construction work to be done out in the bay came in January 1967 with a late phone call. 'Mr Robinson', the voice at the other end of the line said in a friendly tone, 'I've been given your name on good authority. I am told that you know almost every inch of Morecambe Bay, and you seem to be the man we are looking for. Would it be possible for me to come along with a colleague in the next few days for some advice?'

'Aye, it'll be all right, but you'll have to make it a bit more specific than that. I go out on to the sands at different times of the day and night, so if you'll hang on a minute, I'll look at the tide table, to tell you when it would be best for you to come.'

Two days later, at the time arranged, a Land Rover drew up outside Guide's Farm. Two men, one with a briefcase, stepped out, and stopped to look around and out over the bay before coming along the pathway to our front door. I soon learned that our visitors, Bill and Tony, were from the Water Resources Board in Reading; they were preparing a feasibility study for a possible barrage across the bay.

After a cup of tea, we gathered around the table, and one of them spread out a large map of Morecambe Bay. 'Now, Mr Robinson, in the very near future we shall need to take some sand samples from all parts of the bay. Our transport will be a helicopter, and this is where you come in.' Every point where samples were to be taken was marked with a small cross. 'Tell me,' he said, 'is it safe to land almost anywhere out there? Or would we be in danger of landing our helicopter in quicksand?'

'Well, first of all, has the helicopter got wheels or sleds? Because wheels would definitely go into the sand in quite a lot of the places you would be landing on.'

'That's no problem,' Bill said. 'We have skids which will take care of that.' I thought they must mean inflatable skids, which would be ideal for soft, wet sand. 'Right, we've got that one sorted out then.'

They listened carefully as we followed the crosses on the map. 'Mark that as a very bad area,' I would say, and I went on to explain how the rivers, gullies and dykes can change suddenly overnight following high tides or heavy rainfall. We went painstakingly over the whole area. The map was soon looking very different, with several places marked as too dangerous to land on; after an hour or two poring over it, they thanked us for our hospitality and were on their way.

A couple of months later I saw men out in the bay, busy taking small samples of sand from several areas. Soon I had visits from more people wanting information about this part of Morecambe Bay. Some were putting in tenders for the foundation drilling, and wanted to know all about the sands; as they were with me for so short a time, this was an impossibility, but I gave them all the information I could. Eventually a London firm, a subsidiary of a large construction company, was chosen to do the drilling. Two of the bosses arranged with me to be taken out on the sands by tractor.

They arrived on time, and I already had my tractor started up as I didn't want to keep them waiting. They were prepared for any kind of weather, taking from the boot of their car knee boots, leggings, oilskins and a helmet each. They carried with them maps which they kept looking at as we made our way out into the vast expanse of the bay.

I had a wooden platform built out on the back of my tractor, as this was much handier for my job than pulling a trailer all the time. The two men stood on the platform. 'Hold tight,' I said. 'We have to cross the railway line just round the corner here.' The crossing keeper had seen us coming from the window of her house, and as we approached the gates were opened for us. Straight over we went and down the ramp on to the sands. I took it steady, knowing that the two men on the back of my tractor were not used to such rough riding.

I showed them why I would have to make over to the east to give a wide berth to a very soft place, and then back to the west again, pointing out the different types of sand. Some areas were too rough to attempt to drive a tractor over them. Occasionally they asked me to stop, and jumped off the back of the tractor. Referring to their maps, they fired questions at me. 'Where is that place?' 'Is this a good area?' 'Are there many areas which change frequently?' Then they paddled up and down on the sand. After a time they seemed satisfied, although to my mind they had not seen much, not having gone right out into the bay; they decided that we should make our way back home. At this stage, I had no idea what they were planning, or what part I was to play in it.

We returned to Guide's Farm where we sat over a cup of tea chatting about their next move. First, access to the shore and a base to work from would have to be found. Flookburgh was chosen as a base, and since I knew the place well, and most of the people who lived there, we all travelled round by car to make enquiries. I took them to West Plain Farm and introduced them to the farmer, who invited them to have a look round. The farm was close to the shore, with a small plot of land on the other side of the road which would be ideal for their purposes. We were asked inside; an agreement was soon reached, and we left, well satisfied.

Back home we discussed the preparations needed before any start could be made on the work out in the bay. Offices would have to be errected, together with site huts, cabins for the workers and a hut for stores and all the equipment which would be needed. Electricity had to be laid on and the telephone brought in. Luckily there was a tap and fresh water already there; toilets would have to be built. All this had to be done before work on the sands could begin.

I was thanked for all the help I had given and paid well for the time I had spent with the two men, who asked whether I would help them out again from time to time. Nothing definite was arranged at this stage, as I was busy enough with my fishing, but I told them that I didn't mind taking them out on the sands provided I was given some notice. Whatever took place on the sands interested me, and we left it at that. They went away full of confidence in their project.

As I went about my fishing, occasionally I would take the longer route round by road to Flookburgh, just to pass the new site and to see what progress was being made. I would fish my nets, leaving them set for the next tide, and come home across the sands.

Soon I began to make a regular habit of going round this way, and saw that permanent staff had been installed and were waiting for the drilling equipment to be brought up from London to their new base. Meanwhile, the men were making themselves useful by improving the road across the marsh. Lorry-loads of stone were ordered from the local quarries, and a large concrete base was laid at the end of the marsh, where the sand begins. I wondered what this could be for, but I was soon to find out. Bridges were being built over the small gullies which we fishermen had just splashed through on our tractors for years. I could see that things were really moving now. Weeks had gone by and it was getting well into June.

At last I received a telephone call from Northolt in Middlesex, from the drilling manager, followed by a letter asking if I would be willing to help him. He hoped to start work out in the bay in early August. A site agent was coming up in the next few days and he and his wife needed somewhere to stay. Luckily I knew of a place in Grange which suited them well. Then drillers arrived and also found accommodation locally. There was quite a stir in the village.

As work progressed I was needed more often, sometimes to take a couple of technicians out to the line of the proposed barrage. After going out with me when tides were low, and the sand firm and dry in the higher areas, they began to gain confidence — too much confidence, in fact. Arriving down at the site one day I found that the site agent, along with some of his technicians, had ventured out on to the sands in one of their own ex-army wagons, following the tracks made by my tractor a day or so previously. What they did not realise was that the tides were going to rise; if they continued going out on their own, thinking that everything was simple and straightforward, they might very soon learn a tough lesson.

The next time I was asked to go down to the site I noticed a huge circular concrete platform was finished and wagons carrying steel girders of various lengths and sizes were unloading there. Soon the first drilling tower was being assembled. Now I knew the purpose of the concrete platform.

It seemed to me that I ought now to work on a more regular basis, or I might just as well carry on with my fishing. It has to be one or the other, I thought as I walked over to the site office. 'Good morning,' I said to the agent. 'Morning, Mr Robinson. What's the earliest time you can get us out on to the sands?'

'Well, it all depends which area you want to go into.' Leaning over the table, I glanced at a map of the bay with marks and numbers — A6, A7 and so on — representing boreholes. I knew of all the areas where drilling was going to take place, as I had been over them many times. They had been marked out earlier by the surveyors, and wooden stakes put in the sand.

'Could you take the two of us along to this point here?' He put his finger on a spot on the map — A1. I hesitated for a moment, knowing that we could have got to any of the other marked points more easily than to this one. It was in a very low area way over to the west side of the bay, near to the main channel, the River Leven. In this part of the bay, the tide ebbed late and came in sooner, leaving only about four hours of working time. The force of the tide, both outgoing and incoming, was here at its worst and most dangerous. Now I had seen the new drilling tower getting nearer to completion each day. My own belief was that it would never stay upright out there. But they ought to know what they were doing, and whether it would work.

Next I was asked to find some local lads to work on the rigs, so at first half a dozen lads from Flookburgh started at the site. The first job for one of them was to help me to mark a route out on the sands, putting in wooden stakes about a hundred yards apart. We had to wrap each stake around with material of brilliant 'Dayglo' orange colour so that they could be seen in the dark when the tractor lights caught them, as well as acting as markers during daylight hours. The route would be seen even in the fog. At last, the whole route to the site where the drilling tower was to be erected was marked out, and the day and time came for the big move.

Two bulldozers with caterpillar tracks, massive crawler machines, D6s and D7s, had been brought in from a local plant hire firm to tow the drilling tower over the sands. Long wire ropes were shackled from each tractor to the front corners of the huge tower. Eighty feet high, it was constructed of iron girders, with four large hollow metal wheels similar to the front wheel of the old-fashioned steamroller. Although it could be towed quite easily on a level sand, change of direction was a bit of a problem. One bulldozer had to take the strain while the other one slackened off tension. Stops were frequent on the rough, nobbly sand, and with the constant changing of direction we found that nearly all the nuts and bolts were working loose: it took us quite a long time to tighten them up. We also found that the friction caused by the large wheels rubbing against the girders made the metal very warm. By this time we were feeling slightly anxious, for we knew that even if things went without any snags it would take us most of the time between tides to get the tower to its site, a distance of four miles.

But we just managed it, and in spite of everything the tower stood safely, ready to be put into its final position. All this time I had been leading the way with my old tractor. Following at the rear was an ex-army vehicle, four-wheel drive, driven by one of the drillers and carrying the bosses and the other drillers and labourers. They had brought long metal 'matts' to the site — perforated sheets of strong metal, approximately 10ft long by 8ft wide, of the type used in the last war to enable transport to drive over boggy areas without getting stuck. These were laid on the sand to carry the wheeled vehicles over the worst places, and could then be picked up and moved forward. They were eventually to be put under the tower.

Orders were being given as we drew near to the last few yards. The army truck went ahead and then halted. Now the men were flitting about like fleas. I kept my tractor clear and walked over to the spot where the caterpillar tractors were to pull the drilling tower on to the metal matts. The matts were moved about until they were in the correct positions, then instructions were given to the caterpillar drivers to take the strain and slowly ease the tower forward into place. 'Easy does it! Steady! STOP!' came the cries of the gaffer. He was all smiles now, probably thinking that the worst part was over.

When I looked at my watch, I realised that we had only just enough time to get out of this low area with the caterpillars, as they could not go as fast as my old tractor and the army wagon.

Our outward tracks were still showing clearly, so I told the drivers to be making along them. They would soon be on much higher ground where they would be clear of the tide for a long time. After doing a few necessary jobs, we others caught them up. These caterpillar tractors intrigued me: they could go almost anywhere. I stayed alongside them now because dusk was closing in. The army wagon raced over the sands for home and we could see the spray from its wheels until it was right out of sight.

By the time we reached base, everyone except the boss had gone home. We parked our vehicles for the night, then I was called over to the office to confirm times for the next day and to discuss what we were to expect. As the tide comes in twice in twenty-four hours, we should miss the night tide. Tomorrow we should not be able to leave base until two-thirty in the afternoon, but then we ought to be able to go straight out to the rig without any problem. The bosses decided that we should all travel in the army wagon: I was to leave my tractor at the site.

As the next morning passed, everyone was anxious to see how the rig had stood up to the force of the tide. This seemed to be the topic of conversation. I had my own opinion, based on past experiences, but I was simply there with a job to do — a responsible one too, as it turned out.

The time came for us to set off out to the drilling rig. Everyone climbed aboard the army wagon — the drilling manager, the site agent, drillers and their second men, as they were called — a wagon load of us! We held tight as we heard the engine start up, knowing that the ride across the stretch of marsh was going to be a bumpy one, but once out on the sands it was not bad going, and much more comfortable than my old tractor. Perhaps not as reliable, though, I was thinking — as they indeed were to find out later on.

First one of us then another looked out from under the cover of the wagon to see if we could catch sight of the rig. I had a feeling that something was wrong as it came into view. It looked to me as if it was leaning at quite an angle. I pointed this out to the site manager, who was alongside me. 'No, Cedric, optical illusion,' he said. 'Optical illusion, my eye,' I replied. I was used to looking long distances over the sands, and I was sure that the tower was no longer upright; no one could convince me otherwise. The route was well marked all the way, so the driver had no worries on that score and we were soon nearing the rig. I had in my mind's eye just what we should see when we got there, so asked the driver not to go too near, since the tide would have scoured round the rig as it does with anything left on the sand. Even an old tin will have the sand washed away from round it.

After finding that the rig was indeed at an angle, we were unable to get on to it. The tide had scoured round it to such an extent that it was now sitting in a huge waterlogged hole. Not only had sand been taken from around the rig, it had also been washed from underneath, so the whole structure had dropped down the depth of its wheels. The bosses made a quick survey, then decided that if it was possible to straighten up the rig, they might still be able to drill from it. Now for action. Decisions had to be made quickly as we had only four hours between tides. Most of us would have to return to base, leaving only two men out there. They could do nothing at this stage.

Everyone at base was waiting to hear our news, but it was not for us to publicise or criticise, so we gave them the bare facts and waited for our instructions. I was to take the two drivers with their caterpillars out to the rig as quickly as possible. This was going to be a race against time. I checked my tractor for fuel and oil, then drove out of the yard and over the marsh, followed by the two caterpillars.

In the meantime, several lorry-loads of stone had been ordered from a local quarry. As soon as the caterpillars were safely at the site I returned to base to meet the drivers from the quarry. They had been on the marsh before but this time they were actually to go out on the sands, which was a new experience for them. I knew I could get them out there safely, but the salt water in the shallow dykes which we had to go through would play havoc with their braking systems, and once they were back on the road they would have to be extra careful.

The route was easy to follow, the wheelmarks showing from our earlier trip, so I could keep an eye on the drivers and give them some idea of what they would have to do when we reached the rig. I drove backwards and forwards to make sure they were alright. It was like an army convoy. I told them that on no account must they stop on the sands with their load on or their wheels would sink; although the two caterpillars were on hand, they had another job to do. The first lorry driver was asked to get as near as possible to the scoured hole round the rig to tip in his load. I watched the sand quiver as the stone disappeared. A caterpillar tractor was ready to move in to push the stone into the hole. The lorries went round in circles, not daring to stop, keeping clear of each other's wheelmarks so as not to soften up all the sand around the rig. It was an impossible job: a load of stone went nowhere, just disappearing into the gaping hole.

With the amount of stone we had available, and with time running out, we decided to work on one side only, instead of trying to fill in all round, so that we could get on to the rig to see what damage had been done. After a quick inspection, the boss thought that it would be possible — or at least worth a try — to attach long wire cables from a position high up on the structure of the rig. This was at last done, and everyone stood back.

Instructions were clearly given for the two caterpillars to take up the slack of the wires. Steadily, making sure they both pulled evenly together, they started to move; but the suction in the sand around the base of the rig had too strong a hold and would not release it, even to the power of the two caterpillars. The result was catastrophic.

As the eighty-foot-high tower and its equipment broke into pieces and hurtled to the ground, everyone ran for their lives. The noise was terrible, as metal girders and steel sections were breaking up, with one part crashing against another. It was very frightening, but no one was hurt. All we could do now was salvage anything we could easily lay our hands on, and this as quickly as possible. Time was short. The caterpillars must be first on the way home, then the lorry drivers, who all this time had been slowly moving round, not daring to stop. I knew they would be only too glad to go. I jumped on my tractor, ready to lead the convoy to higher and safer ground. It was almost dark by now, and we had to use our lights to see the tracks and markers. One elderly chap, a wagon driver who had lived all his life in the area, said to me, 'Well, lad, I've often wondered what it was like out there, but now I've seen it, yance is enough for me' — meaning he wouldn't go out there again at any price!

We all reached base safely. The lorry drivers thanked me for my help and drove off to their homes. We parked the rest of the vehicles for the night, and I made my way to the office as usual. I had already worked out the times at which we could go out on to the sands the following day; but as there was a lot of valuable equipment where the rig had collapsed I was asked to go with a strong lad from the village, following the next tide, to guard the rig from any would-be pirates. This meant going out in the middle of the night. I took my tractor, and Boxer — that was my mate's nickname — took a tractor and trailer; while we were there we were going to salvage whatever we could.

We had not been at the rig very long when I could see lights coming towards us out of the night. As they drew nearer, we heard the noise of a tractor engine, and then voices. The visitors must have been surprised to find someone already there. On seeing Boxer, who was as strong as an ox, they changed their minds, turned their tractor round sharpish and made off into the darkness. If there had been any trouble my mate could easily have dealt with them; but we weren't looking for a fight, and it didn't come to that. We never found out who they were. We had a flask of coffee and a few sandwiches with us, and now we could relax for a short while and have a natter over our drinks. Before long, daylight would break and we would be better able to see what we could salvage before the turn of the tide.

We got on well with the job, then began to think about making tracks for home. The tide couldn't be far away, so we knew we had better get moving. Piece after piece had been dragged from the heap of twisted metal and loaded into the trailer. Smaller pieces and some equipment were packed on to the back of the tractors, and we made our way home. It was still very early. I looked at my watch — a quarter to seven. The sand was very flat for the first mile or so, and we made good going. The sooner we got back the better, for we would be able to get a few hours sleep before the next tide ebbed. By my reckoning that would be about half past three that afternoon.

The base was quiet as we parked the tractors. It was too early for anyone to have started work, so I dropped Boxer off on my way home, arranging to pick him up about one o'clock, after I had had something to eat. Later, of course, everyone wanted to know how we had fared during our night out on the sands. When we told them of our visitors, there was a great deal of speculation as to who the would-be pirates were, but it had been too dark for us to see where they went.

The salvage operation began. This was to be our final visit to the broken-down rig, and the last to that particular area for a long time. I was asked to accompany a bulldozer with wire ropes, and two tractors with trailers to load up whatever we could salvage. We hoped to clear the area completely this time. The power of the bulldozer was amazing. The wire ropes were fastened to the girders which were pulled clear in no time by the huge machine. Eventually everything that could be saved had been dragged out: all that was left was the gaping hole and a small patch of stone.

We coupled up the bulldozer to the long girders and set off on the return journey. I stayed alongside the bulldozer as the driver had to take it very slowly with his load. The girders gouged great furrows in the sand, slowing our progress still further. Time was slipping by and I waved the tractor drivers to go on ahead. 'Follow the tracks,' I shouted to them. 'Don't try to take any short cuts either: there's plenty under the sand with trying that!'

After a while, I realised we could not make it with this load; the tide would be coming before we manged to get out. So I suggested to the driver that we take the girders up on to higher ground and leave them to be collected later. After all, they were not much good for anything except scrap. The tide would not scour round them on the higher ground, so we unloaded them on a rise and left them, in order to make the base safely. The girders could be brought back next day, when we should have all the time between the tides for the job.

I had thought that, with the disaster of the day before, the whole team would have been disheartened, but the spirit and determination of those lads was wonderful to see. They were not going to allow even such a major setback to prevent the progress of the survey.

10 Taming the Bay

W.E.Swale, in his book *Grange-over-Sands: The Story of a Gentle Township* (1969), describes the work of the survey and the problems of the task in which I became so closely involved:

> Towns north of a line from Hest Bank to, say, Ulverston, face the possible construction of a barrage which would drastically alter their physical surroundings. The object of the original scheme was merely to carry a railway line running to Carlisle and Scotland. Since then, other objectives are in mind — a shorter rail and road route to Barrow, along the top of the dam, a source of cooling water for electricity power stations, land reclamation and, above all, water storage. If it does nothing else, the present 'feasability study' has aroused great interest and been a minor source of local employment. The study, estimated to cost around £500,000 and to be finished in 1971, is proceeding under the overall direction of the Water Resources Board in Reading. The combined skill of a number of specialist firms is being called on so that every conceivable aspect of a complex problem may be exhaustively examined. Consulting Engineers are dealing with constructional work, surveyors have made aerial and hydrographic observations, experts in Soil Mechanics have sunk over 35 boreholes, reaching depths of over 300 feet. A scale model of the waters and shores of Morecambe Bay has been made in which simulated tides will, it is hoped, predict the long term effects of the barrage, as far down as Barrow harbour. It is certain that all these bay explorers will have read accounts of the extraordinary high tide of 27 December 1857, which exceeded by twelve feet anything ever recorded before or since; or of the great gale of 27 February 1903, when, in the early morning hours, the down mail train was blown over as it was crossing the Leven viaduct, fortunately without loss of life. These incidents prove that Morecambe Bay will not be easily tamed.

He was right about the difficulties, as our first disastrous attempt had already proved. But the work went on.

New plans had to be thought out and many journeys were made out on to the sands, trying out different ideas and techniques. In some areas it was decided to use stone as the foundation on which to build the steel scaffolding. In other places where the tidal flow was stronger, it was found that mattresses of perforated sheet steel fixed on girders laid over sheets of hessian were the most effective.

My chief job was choosing routes out to new areas, marking them and visiting the drilling rigs with the boss. Mostly I acted as guide. I had nothing to do with the actual drilling. When a new base for a drilling rig was being laid, it was most important that everything possible should be known about sand and tides in the area. This was where my experience of the bay was most useful to the firm. I felt I had a great responsibility for the safety of both personnel and plant. What a good firm and a grand lot of lads these were to work with, too. At first we were nearly all strangers to one another, but as time progressed, we got on very well together.

Scaffold firms were soon busy erecting drilling towers up and down the bay. They had to have information about the flow of the tides in each area where it was proposed to put up a tower. The job was a formidable one, as all their equipment had to be taken out on tractors and four-wheeled trailers, hired from local firms. I marked out routes where I knew the sands would be safe for some time. When I was sure there would be no great change along these routes, I would give the drivers the times of the tides and tell them when they could go out and return in safety; but if the weather was changeable or if there was any chance of fog, I would take them out, guiding them from my tractor. In this way serious trouble was avoided.

However, there was one close shave. I had given one of the lads directions for getting back to our base, telling him to follow my wheel tracks. Unfortunately, another set of tracks had been uncovered by the ebbing tide while we had been working out at the rig, and the driver followed the wrong set, making down the bay into the fast-running tide which was coming up the channel. Boxer and I were on our way home when we spotted him. We turned the tractor in his direction, put on all the speed we had and soon had him back on the right course. 'Whew,' said Boxer, 'we shouldn't have seen him again,

Ced, if we'd not just bin comin past.'

A large number of men was needed to work on the drilling rigs. Plans had to be worked out for getting them out to the rigs and back to the shore. One of the firm's vans was used to bring the men in to base from their homes or digs; my job was to take them out to the drilling platforms on my tractor, between tides, and bring them back to base after their stint was over. In all kinds of weather, it was a most uncomfortable ride for the men, especially when they were tired from their hard work on the rigs. Eventually the firm decided to buy a DUKW, an American ex-army amphibious craft used in the last war as a personnel carrier. It may have been old, but it was comfortable, had six-wheel drive and could get out to any area at speed. It did quite well as a personnel carrier. However, Morecambe Bay is different from other sites where the DUKW would be in deep water right off the shore. Out here in the bay, you could be in the river where the water was fast-flowing and then suddenly find yourself in shallower water; as the front of the vehicle was lighter than the rear end, it would spin us round, and we couldn't solve this problem at first. Eventually we found we had either to go out when the tide was fairly high or wait until the tide had ebbed so that we could go on our wheels.

The large size of the DUKW tempted men to start using it to take all sorts of equipment out to the rigs. I grew more and more worried as I saw bigger and bigger loads being taken out. I felt they were tempting providence.

I was out on the sands very early one morning, taking men out to the two drilling rigs on the west side of the bay just out from Aldingham. Between us and Flookburgh was the fast-flowing River Leven. The DUKW was transporting men and equipment to and from the rigs on the Flookburgh side of the river. On my way back to the shore, I could see it quite clearly, coming out from Flookburgh and speeding towards the rigs I had just left. I knew the tide was coming in, and thought, 'What are those fools doing out there at this time?' It was the top of the flood with big tides running. The vehicle was loaded with scaffolding, and there were half a dozen men on it. They must have mistaken the time of the tide. When the DUKW got into the river the tidal bore hit it and turned it round; with water pouring into the rear end the front was coming up fast. The men were all huddled together at the fore-end, completely at the mercy of the tide. At last, they had the sense to throw the scaffolding off to relieve the weight. The vehicle righted itself, but not before those lads had been scared more than they had ever been scared in their lives.

They had plenty of power to make their way back to Chapel Island, but were now on the wrong side of the River Leven. When they tried to cross the river, the force of the tide turned them round again. They did eventually get away from it helped by the speed of their vehicle, and were able to make back to Flookburgh. Later they told us about their alarming experience, saying that one of the drillers, a coloured lad, went white with fright when he saw the danger they were in. He got his own back on the other lads: he said that they went green!

At home that night, I couldn't stop thinking about this affair. I was afraid they would not be so lucky another time, so I sat down and wrote out a list of the jobs for which I thought it was safe to use the DUKW. Everyone agreed, so a list was put up in the front of the vehicle, and a copy in the office. After that the DUKW was used sensibly, without any more trouble.

Drilling was going on well from the rigs based at Flookburgh, and now more were needed at the other side of the bay. The foreshore at Bolton-le-Sands was chosen for the base from which to start the work of building the new rigs. As soon as they were built the men were brought out from Flookburgh on the DUKW to work on them. The biggest problem was getting the men to the rigs when the tide was at the full in the early morning. To save time, it was decided to take the men round by road to the other side of the bay, where a fisherman I knew well would meet them at the jetty and take them out to the rigs in his boat. I was able to go along with the men and help with the unloading. We found it difficult unloading on to the steel structure of the rigs when the sea was choppy; rough conditions also made it tricky for the men to climb from the boat to the rig. A row of old motor tyres hung at the right height solved the problem to some extent; on fine days, of course, we had no trouble at all. Each rig had an inflatable life-raft, fitted with an outboard engine, in case of emergency, so the safety of the men was well to the fore. There was also a walkie-talkie radio system, which saved a lot of time and could save lives too.

The only occasion when one of the inflatables had to be used was when the men on one of the drilling rigs thought they felt it move. Word was passed to the base by radio, and very soon I was on my way round to the jetty at Morecambe, where I found Ernie in his boat waiting for me. As we neared the rig I could see the three men sitting in the rubber dinghy, anchored to the ramp which leads up to the rig. They were glad to see us: it couldn't have been too pleasant sitting in an open boat, maybe thinking about the rig which had collapsed earlier. We took them back to base, and when the tide had ebbed I took the boss out on my tractor to survey the damage. An extra high tide during the night had scoured round the stone base, although looking at the structure of the rig itself it seemed that very little had happened. When the men felt it move slightly, the tide would have been scouring round the base and the rig would have been straining; this drew the metal casing up out of the sand, causing slight movement of the rig. There was plenty of time to do what was needed to stabilise the structure. Stone was on hand, stockpiled for just such an emergency. As soon as the tide had left the area, work was started on filling in the base. It was soon finished and the lads were able to work on the rig again the following day.

Now that all the rigs were in working order and drilling was going ahead, I could bring my tractor back across the sands to Flookburgh. The river had to be forded, and at that time I knew a good shallow crossing well up in the bay where I could get through quite easily. I should be able to make the first half of the journey in the daylight if I got moving. After fording the river up near Grange, I was glad to be closer to home, for I could see fog coming in fast, rolling up the bay and blotting out all sight of any landmarks; now I had to use my knowledge of the area, as I had no tracks to follow. Although I hadn't very far to go, a short distance on the sands in the fog seems never-ending. I switched on my tractor lights, but they just made the fog and darkness look like a blank wall; I was better without them. I was glad to get up on to higher ground, where finally I came across some tracks on the sand. I got down and had a close look at them. Yes, they were my own tracks. I found a marker I had put in a few days earlier and knew that I was on the way to the marsh. Was I glad to get home that Friday night!

No one went out to the rigs on Saturday or on Sunday. Little did we know that five lads, part-time fishermen, had gone down from Lancaster on Friday evening. They had packed up their sandwiches and a couple of flasks of tea and they went to do a night's fishing. They had two boats in which they sailed down the Lune to the mouth of the river and out into the bay.

It came in foggy and they soon lost their way. They had no compass, and no idea where they were at all. They were too cold to sleep, and too scared, I should think. By the next day all their food had gone. They had a can of water but had to go carefully with that, not knowing how long they would be out there before somebody came to their rescue. Saturday and Sunday came and went; the situation grew more frightening by the minute. It was given out on the radio that five fishermen were missing in Morecambe Bay, but in such fog it was no use any other boats going out. Since the fishermen had no radio with them, they didn't even know whether or not they had been missed.

On Monday morning I had to go out over the bay on my tractor to take some workmen to one of the rigs, about a mile and a half out from Morecambe. I left at six o'clock from Flookburgh; it took longer than usual to reach the rig as the fog was still fairly thick. I landed the men without any trouble and had turned in a wide circle to start the journey back over the bay when I thought I could see what looked like a boat. I knew I could get closer with my tractor, and sure enough, there were two boats with some figures standing round the masts. The water was no more than three feet deep, and I wondered what on earth two boats were doing there. Then it dawned on me that these were the five fishermen lost in the bay. Only that morning I had heard on the radio that they were still missing. I had imagined they would have been much farther out. Well, when I got close to them, I saw that they were as black as the fire-back! This was Monday morning, and they had been out since Friday night. The fishermen recognised me at once, because a couple of months earlier my son and his pal Larry had bought a boat from them, and I had run the two lads round to Lancaster in my car.

'Bloody 'ell, Ced,' they cried as I approached, 'aren't we glad to see thee! Where the 'ell are we?' Now when it is foggy and hazy, you can still see the sun coming up above the haze. I knew exactly where they were, and told them, 'Sail about ten minutes down there,' pointing in the direction they must take. 'And then just make into t'sun, and with a bit of luck, you'll land just about by Morecambe jetty.' They were in boats with a very shallow draught, so I knew they would make it all right. It was all in the newspapers next day. But by gum, it was lucky they saw me that Monday morning.

On Tuesday, I was glad to see the fog had cleared, as there was some equipment needed at short notice on one of the rigs quite close to Morecambe. On this occasion, Ernie was out in the bay fishing for shrimps; but my friend Larry, who is a most obliging chap, had offered to give me a hand if ever I needed help, so I got in touch with him and we soon had the goods aboard his boat. The rig was about half a mile off Morecambe, and we got there without any trouble; but Larry is very daring, and we were a little bit late on the tide.

We unloaded all the equipment, then turned the boat round for home. There was a breeze coming up, and quite a lot of surf; when we got near where the river was ebbing, there was even more surf. Every time I looked round, great rollers were coming over the boat. We were both soaked to the skin. We were too late on the tide, and he wouldn't ease his engine off; the front was right up out of the water. I thought, 'Well, it's sink or swim like this'; I'm no boatman admittedly, but I'd never sailed like this in my life. The front went up and the back went down — I was down on my hands and knees and couldn't stand up, so I got the life jacket from up front and left Larry to look to the sailing of the boat.

As I said, I have never been a boatman, and don't know whether the bows are at the front or the back; but I've travelled over almost every inch of the bay when the tide is out, and know every dyke and hollow in it. Larry yelled to me that he would have to make for Humphrey Head to keep in deep enough water, and as the boat careered towards the Headland I thought, 'Thee bloody well sail for Humphrey Head, Larry, 'cos if tha keeps going, tha'll run aground.' And I was more than glad when I felt the bottom of the boat run on to a sandbank, as otherwise he would have carried on and there's no knowing where we would have ended up. Having let him run aground, I knew exactly where we were: it was the place we called the 'goldmine', because we always got plenty of fish when we had nets out there. We had a five-mile walk home, but I'd rather walk than travel by boat in that way!

The story isn't over yet, though. The next day, Larry wanted me to take him out to the boat on my tractor. I knew, of course, where it had gone aground, but as usual, Larry was late. Eventually we got out from Flookburgh and down to the shore. The boat was right at the top of the 'gold mine'; the tide had just gone past it, but I knew I could go up to it with my tractor. The tide was only about halfway up my wheels, but it was running very fast. So I went in quickly; Larry and our Robert, who had come to give him a hand, both jumped into the boat, and I came back out of the tide and on to the bank to watch them. They had no more sense than to start the engine up, though the tide had only just gone by them! They should have lain at anchor for an hour at least, because the bank went up higher before dropping into the main river. Soon after starting the engine they went straight into a sandbank, which threw them aground yet again, and this time they were broadside on. I could see the current was likely to tip them over.

As for what Larry did next — he should have had a medal for it. He had a plank in the boat; there was a lip round the edge of the boat, and he put the plank under this lip, with the other end of it several feet out over the water, then went out on to it and jumped up and down until the boat was freed. Then he scrambled back in and they sailed off for Grange. It took my breath away to see him prancing on that plank. But, as I said before, Larry has no fear. He certainly wasn't brought up to the danger of the sands as I was. Anyway he got away with it that time.

By the time of this adventure some of the rigs out from Flookburgh had almost finished their drillings, and before long the job of dismantling would have to begin. I had enjoyed the whole period of my employment with the firm, and none of us was looking forward to the day when the survey would come to an end. I can honestly say we had made some sincere friendships; later, from time to time, we had the chance of having a get-together.

In 1972, after five years of study, the Water Resources Board concluded that Morecambe Bay could be used for freshwater storage. Several different schemes were outlined. A full barrage twelve miles long, reaching from Hest Bank near Morecambe to Baycliffe near Aldingham and carrying a dual-carriageway road above it, would cost an estimed £69-73 million. A major disadvantage of this plan would be the probable extent of silting on the seaward side, putting at risk major ports such as Heysham Harbour, Fleetwood and Barrow.

The board did not in fact recommend at that stage whether or not the bay should be developed, and since then the project appears to have been shelved for lack of funds. So all that is now in the past, but it is not forgotten: since all the forms of water storage examined by the board are feasible in engineering terms, sometime in the future the barrage could become a reality. W E Swale examines the prospects:

> If the barrage is ever built, the livelihood of a hardy, modest and extremely knowledgeable race of men will largely disappear. The emergence of a 40 square mile inland lake has exciting possibilities, not only for many kinds of water sport, but also for other types of fishing. The 'broad waters' (as they have for centuries been known in local records) have their hazards. Changes in plant and animal life, notably in the possible growth of sedges and rushes around the shores of the lake, may pose yet unforeseen problems. It is more than likely that the present generation of fishermen may still be able to use their particular skills in the service of subsequent users of (or sufferers from) the great Morecambe Lake.

If all this were to come to pass, my job as Queen's Guide would obviously become obsolete. I should have to learn to tell one end of a boat from another, buy a small fleet and hire them out on the new lake. What a thought! This would seem the only method of earning a living which would remain open to me, but it could never compensate me for my memories of the past. If the Morecambe Bay barrage were to be built in my lifetime, I should lose something which has been part of me all my life — my livelihood, my constant challenge, my second home: the sands.

Appendix A:

The Wildlife of Morecambe Bay

Around Morecambe Bay are various unspoilt areas where there has been very little disturbance since the war ended. This has enabled many species of animal to survive in fairly large numbers. Frogs and toads are frequently seen during the breeding season. The badger, rabbit, hare, stoat and weasel are all fairly common on the wooded slopes around the bay, and the red squirrel has been seen during the last few years. For a time we thought we had lost this lovely little creature.

The wily fox, whose brain is said to be infinitely superior to that of the best domestic dog, will even raid the nets out on the sand when food on the land is scarce. I have seen the tell-tale tracks on the sand leading to my nets, where the fox had taken his fill of the fish.

Moles are continually doing damage in the soft, peaty fields, leaving their 'mole-heaps' looking like a string of small volcanoes across the grass. When caught they are skinned, and the pelts hung up to dry. At one period they were much in demand for fur coats, but the moleskin coat is out of fashion at the present time.

Swallows come to nest in the outbuildings of Guide's Farm every year, and they are always a welcome sight, as they are supposed to bring good luck with them. In any case they are a pleasure to watch, flying in and out of the buildings without fear.

The moorhen is common where there is good cover near the water for nesting, and the plover — or tewit, as the locals call it, from its cry — builds its nest on farmland or on marshy ground around the bay. The eggs used to be much sought-after, as they are counted a delicacy, but the taking of plovers' eggs is now discouraged. The birds are valuable to the farmer, as they eat the water snail on the wet, marshy land which cause liver fluke in sheep, and they are now on the protected list.

It is said that there are some 150 species of bird on Morecambe Bay itself, and birds have been found from as far away as Iceland and Siberia. Whether in spring, when terns can be seen taking whitebait back to their nests to feed their young, or in autumn, when pink-footed and greylag geese, newly arrived from the north for the winter, gather to feed on Foulshaw Marshes north of Arnside viaduct, there is always plenty to interest the enthusiast. Of course, if you are only able to go around the shore of the bay you miss a great deal. I have seen flocks of up to a thousand shelduck feeding out there on the sands, but I always keep well away from the birds so that I will not separate parents from their young — the gulls are always waiting for undefended chicks — or the birds from their rightful feeding grounds.

I have this feeling that they have more right to be there than I have, and they have their place in the scheme of things. The balance of nature is very easily upset; even digging in the sand for bait can kill off a great deal of the minute life on which the birds and other creatures depend for their living.

The shelduck is a very handsome bird with its black, white and chestnut colouring. A few pairs may be seen close in to the shore before the breeding season, shovelling in the sand with their beaks in the way all ducks do.

Another common species is the 'sea-pie' or oyster catcher, a fairly large black and white bird which has been known to live for an amazing twenty-nine years. The fishermen used to set nets on a banking near the shore to catch them; they were skinned, not plucked, and they certainly made a good meal. The nets were set at low tide on what we called the brod, which is where the tide just lapped to. It was no good if it was too light, for the birds would see the nets, which were set on stakes seven or eight feet high, with a good bag. The birds fly low, and quite a number would be caught in this way. The idea was to collect them before the next tide. This is not allowed today: someone once left his nets over the weekend and people saw the birds fluttering out there, so the practice was stopped.

The dunlin are so fascinating that when you are out on the sands, you cannot take your eyes off them. You may be setting your nets when suddenly you will hear the sound of thousands of wings, startling in its intensity. Out there alone, miles from anywhere, you can see them wheeling and turning, the mass of birds forming a cloud forever changing shape. In the sunlight they are so beautiful that you never quite get used to the sight; you have to stop your work for a few minutes to watch. When they are down on the sand feeding, they run like mice, and indeed they are called 'sea-mice' by the fishermen in these parts. Taking off to move to fresh ground, they are closely knit, all together in flight — a miracle to watch as they weave, rise and fall, looking at first glance like a cloud of smoke blowing about in the air. Then, suddenly, the colour changes to silver, giving the impression of a huge mass of tinsel flickering from the sun's reflection. Close to, they fly past with the sound and movement of air, and with such force that it is hard to realise they have no mechanical means of propulsion. When they turn, it is as one, so close and yet not touching. Like the genie from a magic lamp is this cloud of little birds, now silver, now black.

Seagulls can often be seen treading the sand to bring the shellfish up to the surface, in just the same way as we use the jumbo. I'm sure that whoever thought of rocking a plank back and forth on the sand to bring the cockles up must first have watched the seagulls doing the job in such an efficient way.

Many a time, when we have been throwing shrimp husks out on the sands for the gulls to eat, I have seen not just the odd bird but quite a few from time to time, with just one leg or one good leg and a stump; and I have also seen a gull with a tin can hanging from its leg. I think what must happen is that, when there is no fish waste available, the gulls probably fly inland to some rubbish tip. There a bird may land, for example, on a tin with the lid partly cut open, and get its foot caught; the tin closes like a trap, and after the bird has been flying around like this for some time the tin will eventually cut through the leg and the bird will lose its foot. But the bird takes no hurt on account of the salt water which encourages the wound to heal up.

There was one old seagull we used to see always waiting for the waste: it seemed to have been there for years. It didn't seem able to fly, but used to flap its wings and run along as if it were too heavy to take off. It must have been a greedy old bird, as it was always there. We used to call it Hitler.

There are many bird casualties of which no one is aware, but one day Olive actually saw a seagull fly into a passing train. As soon as the train had passed by, she climbed over the wall and on to the railway line, where she could see the bird fluttering on its side between the lines. It was bleeding from an injury to one of its wings. When she brought it into the house, we found the wing was not broken, but the skin was torn and it must have been badly bruised. We have a small stone building in the orchard where we felt that it would be safe from marauding cats and dogs. We lined a wooden box with grass and hay, which the seagull readily accepted, and a large bowl of water was placed nearby. Every day for six weeks Olive fed the bird with whitebait, fish roes and sprats; it grew gradually stronger and began coming to the door to meet her. It became so tame that it would take the fish from her fingers.

As its strength returned, we let it out into the orchard for a bit of exercise each day, and soon it was trying the damaged wing. Olive decided it was time to take the bird down to the shore and see if it could fend for itself. She stood on the ramp a few feet above the sand and gently let the bird go. It flew for about fifty yards, then settled and started to tread the sand and pick up the shellfish and sandworms that abound there. It was quite able to look after itself now, so she made her way home.

Next day a friend came knocking on the door: 'Look what I've found walking up the road. It must have been making back here!' It was the seagull. We kept it for another couple of weeks before letting it go again, and this time it went winging its way right out of sight. It was back with its own kind, and it came to us no more.

When Diane was about eleven years old, she often used to come to the beach to wait for me on my return from the nets. She loved to ride on the tractor across the railway, when the gates would be opened specially for us. Sometimes there would be the added thrill of waiting for a train to go by before the crossing keeper could open the gates. On such a day, Diane was waiting on the beach when, just as I was coming up to her, she saw four little ducklings plaintively calling for their mother who never came. She called to me and we collected the little fluffy creatures and we carried them home with us. They could only have been a few days old, and our first thoughts centred on how to keep them warm. Olive decided that the best thing would be the electric clothes drier. We put them on a cosy blanket in the drier, which had to be turned on and off at regular intervals to avoid extremes of temperature. This had to be done even through the night, of course. We fed them on pieces of worms and tiny scraps of raw fish, and they grew and were very content with their new 'mother', sleeping peacefully between feeding times.

This went on for a few weeks. We used to fill a shallow bath with water, and as they grew, they enjoyed swimming around. They had a wonderful time diving for little pieces of bread Diane threw in for them. But as time went on, we realised they were needing their freedom — they were starting to fly around the living room! So we took them down to the beach — not four little balls of fluff now, but four young mallards able to fend for themselves, and no longer in need of us.

I remember as a lad going with my pal to Chapel Island looking for birds' nests. They were mainly shelduck up there. I've seen shelduck with young ones running about on the sands, but rarely have I seen mallards with their young on the shore, though I have seen them swimming on the tide when they were quite small. It seems natural for the shelduck to have their young running on the beach, but I think the mallards like to nest well away from the water, and more often nearer to fresh water than to sea water.

I occasionally set some nets deeper than we usually use — trap nets, we call them — for flukes. They are more meshes deep, with a lot of spare bag, and are on longer stakes than normal — more like the nets we used to catch the sea-pies in the old days. The nets are set on a high bank, at night; a good strong breeze is favourable, as the fish cannot see the meshing in choppy, murky waters and get trapped, usually by the gills. I have caught a seagull in this way from time to time, but once I caught something really unusual. It was a storm petrel — one of Mother Carey's Chickens, as they are known. I took it home and we fed it on cod-liver oil and whitebait, which I was catching at that time. It did quite well, and when it had recovered we released it. It must have been blown off its course in a gale, for although, as I have said, we are used to seeing many kinds of birds in our area, a storm petrel in Morecambe Bay is a rare occurrence indeed.

The wide variety of plant habitats — woodland, meadow, marsh and seashore — to be found in the bay make it a real treasure-land for the botanist. Familiar country flowers such as the bluebell, primrose, cowslip, violet, meadowsweet and ramsons grow side by side with less common plants like deadly nightshade; herb paris (*Paris quadrifolia*), which is quite rare, can be found in the woods.

Walking with a friend along the rocky shoreline from Guide's Farm for a distance of about 250yd, I found the following plants growing:

Aaron's rod *(Verbascum thapsus)*
birdsfoot trefoil *(Lotus corniculatus)*
brown-rayed knapweed *(Centaurea jacea)*
burnet rose *(Rosa spinosissima)*
caraway *(Carum carvi)*
common St John's-wort *(Hypericum perforatum)*
corn mint *(Mentha arvensis)*
dog daisy *(Chrysanthemum leucanthemum)*
dog rose *(Rosa canina)*
golden-rod *(Solidago virgaurea)*
herb robert *(Geranium robertianum)*
lesser yellow trefoil *(Trifolium dubium)*
meadow buttercup *(Ranunculus acris)*
rose-bay *(Chamaenerion angustifolium)*
sea aster *(Aster tripolium)*
sea pea *(Lathyrus japonicus)*
sea thrift *(Armeria maritima)*
stonecrop *(Sedum acre)*
upright hedge parsley *(Torilis japonica)*
wild carrot *(Daunus carota)*

Another speciality of the area is the edible plant samphire *(Salicornia herbacea)*, though this is not as common as it used to be. Thirty to forty years ago, there were large areas of samphire growing close to the shore around the bay. It was gathered by the fishermen, who took it home in clean sacks to be washed and then despatched it by train to the Lancashire towns, in the same way as cockles. Samphire can be eaten boiled and eaten plain, or used as a relish after being pickled in vinegar. It is also a great favourite with the widgeon!

Morecambe Bay is also notable for its fossils, which are quite easy to find in the limestone rocks on the beach and on Humphrey Head. One can find coral masses, and of course there is a wide variety of shells of all sizes.

Appendix B:

Information on the Walks and Other Activities

How to contact the guides

Mr C Robinson
Guide's Farm
Cart Lane
Grange-over-Sands
Cumbria
tel 044 84 2165

Mr A Butler
Levens House
Canal Foot
Ulverston
Cumbria
tel 0229 54156

Length of walks

The longer walks, from Hest Bank near Morecambe to Grange-over-Sands, can vary in distance from eight miles one week to twelve another week, owing to frequent changes in the course of the river. The shorter walk from Grange to Arnside is a distance of about four miles as the crow flies, but again there is the river to contend with, and as we are not crows most of the crossings are made in a roundabout way.

The time taken for the walks also varies. The longer walk can take anything from three and a half to four and a quarter hours. Last season, on the Grange to Arnside route, it took us about an hour to the river, a further three-quarters of an hour following the coastline back up to the point where we could leave the sands, and then half an hour more to the railway station at Arnside.

Clothing for walks

This of course will vary according to personal taste and the weather, but do make sure to bring some warm clothing and a waterproof, as conditions can change rapidly out in the bay in even the hottest weather. Shorts, or an old pair of jeans or trousers, are probably the most suitable; you are going to get wet to some extent, so don't be too particular about the way you look.

With regard to footwear, I prefer to go barefoot as my feet are hardened to the sands, but for most people this would be very hard going. Whether you choose to wear plimsolls, training shoes or strong shoes, you are well advised to wear thick socks to prevent your heels from becoming chafed.

Hampsfell Hospice

On the fells behind Grange, at a height of 750ft, stands Hampsfell Hospice, affording glorious views of Morecambe Bay, the mountains of the Lake District and the valley of the Kent. A mountain indicator helps the visitor to identify Scafell, Helvellyn, Skiddaw and the various other Lakeland peaks. The walk up to the hospice, along steep, well-worn paths, is a very popular one, and is often added to the cross-bay walks for those who still have the energy. The building was originally erected to give shelter to wanderers lost on the fells; an inscription, dated 1846, reads as follows:

This Hospice has an Open Door
Alike to welcome rich and poor;
A roomy seat for young and old
Where they may screen them from the cold.

Three windows that command a view
To North, to West and Southward too;
A flight of steps requireth care,
The roof will show a Prospect rare.

Mountain and vale you thence survey,
The winding streams and Noble Bay,
The sun at noon the shadow hides
Along the East and Western sides.

The blue and lofty mountain sides,
The Noble Bay and stealthy tides —
That treach'rous creep along the sand,
Or lordly dash upon the strand.

A lengthened chain holds guard around,
To keep the cattle from the ground;
Kind reader freely take your pleasure,
But do no mischief to my Treasure.

Maps of the area

Ordnance Survey sheet SD 37/47
Grange-over-Sands
Scale: 1:25,000 (4cm = 1km, or 2½in = 1 mile)

Ordnance Survey sheet 97
Kendal and Morecambe
Scale: 1:50,000 (2cm = 1km, or 1¼in = 1 mile)

Further information about the area

Morecambe Bay and its surroundings, together with the Lake District, are very much a holiday area, and the Tourist Information Offices of the Cumbria Tourist Board can give full details of places to visit, activities, entertainments and so on. The Grange office is situated at

Victoria Hall, Main Street, Grange-over-Sands (tel 044 84 4331).

Contact the National Trust's Regional Information Officer, at Broadlands, Borrans Road, Ambleside, Cumbria (tel 096 63 3003), for more details of NT properties and nature trails in the region.

Not to be missed is the Theatre in the Forest, Grizedale (tel 022 984 291), where festivals, music, drama and lectures can be enjoyed throughout the year.

Preview of Lakeland is a mine of information; it is published three times a year, in spring, summer and autumn, by Preview Publications, 58 Main Street, Flookburgh, Grange-over-Sands, Cumbria (tel 044 853 625). The very latest details of what to do and see locally can be obtained from the *Westmorland Gazette* (Stricklandgate, Kendal, Cumbria, tel 0539 20555) and the *Barrow News and Mail* (Abbey Road, Barrow-in-Furness, Cumbria).

The Lakeland Rose Show

In 1962 the first Lakeland Rose Show, the new showcase of the north for horticulturalists, was held on a lovely site adjoining Guide's Farm. The magnificent show exceeded all expectations; it was clear that a larger site would have to be found, and Mr and Mrs Cavendish at nearby Holker Hall offered the committee the use of the deer park of their popular stately home. Here the show has been held ever since, on the second weekend of July each year.

In 1973 the show hosted the Royal National Rose Society's Northern Show, and has done so regularly since. The National Sweet Pea Society has also visited with its Northern Show.

The show was opened in 1976 by Princess Margaret, and in that same year Fryers of Knutsford named a rose in its honour — 'Lakeland'. In 1979, Princess Michael of Kent came to open the show and Harkness & Co named a rose after her.

The magnificent displays in the great marquee, floral art marquee and other sections under cover are supported by an exciting, varied and interesting programme of outside events which include military bands, flying displays, fashion shows, floral art demonstrations, gymnastic displays and aerial acrobatics, with such top attractions as the Royal Air Force Red Arrows; plus, of course, the beautiful gardens and home of past Dukes of Devonshire.

The cross-bay swim

In addition to its walks, Morecambe Bay also boasts a cross-bay swim, which has taken place every year since 1907 with the exception only of the years of World War II.

Prior to 1907, young men swimming and diving off the West End Pier around the beaches of Morecambe had considered the possibility of swimming across the bay, and in the early summer of that year a boatload of them sailed over to Grange and attempted to swim back. They were unsuccessful, but were convinced that a better swimmer would be able to complete the crossing. Arrangements were made with a prominent swimmer of that time, Professor Stearne of Manchester, and on 13 July 1907 he completed the swim in 3hr 45min 41sec. A collection was taken on Morecambe promenade, 75 per cent of the takings being given to Professor Stearne and the other 25 per cent used to assist in the future formation of the Cross-Bay Swimming Association.

Since that time, the event has attracted long-distance swimmers from all over the country, especially those with ambitions to swim the Channel. It is not an easy swim, covering a distance of between nine and eleven miles, according to the tides, and having to contend with the freshwater currents entering the bay, all of which makes it good training.

The first amateur to swim the bay was J.McMahon of Preston, on 26 August 1907. The first Bay Champion was Brieley Law of Chadderton, who took this honour in 1907-9, 1924, 1929 and 1932, completing his last swim in 1948. Henry Taylor, also of Chadderton, set a record time of 2hr 2min in 1914; this has never been bettered. Charles Daly of Manchester held the record of 26 swims until 1947, but this was broken two years ago by Cmdr C.G. Forsberg, OBE, of Otter Swimming Club, who completed 27 swims in the years 1951-1978.

Tom Blower, Bay Champion 1935-8, was the first Morecambe Bay swimmer to swim the Channel; since then many people have completed both swims, and two Morecambe Bay swimmers, Michael Read and Kevin Murphey, have swum the Channel two ways and are attempting to do it three ways. Since the war, ladies have been prominent in both Morecambe Bay and Channel swims, among them Eileen Fenton (Dewsbury), Brenda Fisher (Grimsby) and Dorothy Perkins (Bradford).

When the bay swims were first organised, it was easy to arrange pilots and rowing boats, but since 1946 it has been difficult to obtain clinker-built boats and canoes are now used instead. These are good for setting a course, but the canoeists are not able to pull a swimmer on board, which means that more escort boats and runabout boats have to patrol among the swimmers. The councils of Morecambe and Grange have always been very good in publicising the event and providing dressing accommodation, and press reports too have given the swim a good deal of publicity.

Since 1975, the cross-bay swims have been organised by the British Long-Distance Swimming Association.

SAMPHIRE

Short Glossary of Terms used by the Fishermen of Morecambe Bay

bar	fording place in the channel
beds	marks left on the sand after using the jumbo
brack	a place where sand has broken away because of the undermining currents of the moving tide
brod	where the tide laps to; or, sticks and rubbish carried in by the tide
channel	a deep bed or groove in which water runs; frequently used of the river channel
cramb	a hand-held, three-pronged tool, like a curved fork, used for picking up cockles
dooak	to flop down into the sand (of a fluke)
drag	a strong rake used for gathering cockles when they are plentiful
dyke	a shallow area of water
flow-hole	an area where the sand has formed a series of deep waves, either in or out of the water
fluke, flounder	a flat fish similar to plaice
foxfire	the phosphorescent glowing of the water at night
glemp	to look at
good show	the imprint of a large number of flukes in the sand
good tails	a good catch
gully	a hollow, freshwater drain-off from the land
have net	small hand net used by the Flookburgh fishermen for catching salmon
hen-pennies	small pink shellfish (bivalves)
jumbo	a two-handled plank which is rocked to and fro on the sand to bring the cockles to the surface
lave net	type of net used when catching salmon in the River Lune
marsh	sea-washed turf, usually round coastal areas, often grazed by sheep

melgrave	hole scoured out by the incoming tide, usually on the edge of the channel, in which sand is deposited on the ebb tide
muck	all types of seaweed
mussel fork	a fork with two prongs 3-4in long used to prize mussels from the rocks
old spot	a stretch of deep water with very little movement
picking	separating the husk or shell from the shrimp
rank	plentiful
riddle	round sieve used when cockling to sort out the very small fish, which are left to grow on for the next season
skeer, scar	a large, permanent area of stone, sand and gravel found a short distance offshore in tidal areas
stake net	a net attached to stakes in the sand, with a good bag, in which the fish are caught between the meshes.
take stek	to stop and refuse to budge (of a horse)
wheaat	very young small cockles

For generations, fishermen have said of soft sand or quicksand, 'It'll mire a cat,' meaning that even a light, nimble cat would get fast in such an area.

Local Dialect Words and Pronunciations of Flookburgh

Flookburgh folk are traditionally supposed to be able to speak with Icelanders, their language having much in common.

aw reet	all right
aye	yes
blah-ing	blowing
boo-at	boat
bree-ad	bread
brust	breast
cald	cold
clee-as	clothes
coo-al	coal
cu theesell here	come here
doo-er	door
down't	down the . . .
dusta nah?	do you know?
ee-ad	head
efter	after
fire-sud	fireside
flee-ak	fluke
ganza	jersey
ghuss	grass
gitten	got
gu'lad	good lad
gut	big
guyn	going
hesta?	have you?
ista reet?	are you ready?
ivver	ever
kae-ak	cake
lakeing	playing
lee-ad	load
leet	light
loo-af	loaf
luckster	look
lyle	small
mar	more
mee-at	meat
mebby	maybe
misel	myself
nah, nay	no
neet	night
nobbot	only
noo-as	nose

noo-at	note
nowt	nothing
nudder	another
oor theer	over there
ousta doin?	how are you doing?
owt	anything
pay-ap-er	paper
pund	pound
reet	right
roo-ad	road
roo-ep	rope
secks	bags
sin	seen
sister theer	look there
sote	salt
stay-ak	stake
summet	something
tae-abble	table
tay-as	toes
tha	you
tha'll	you will
tha nahs	you know
tha's	you have
tha wot?	what did you say?
theer	there
to gar	to go
turble	terrible
up t'village	up to the village
vara	very
wa-a-rm	warm
watter	water
wedder	weather
wesh	wash
willta?	will you?
wrang	wrong
yam	home
yance	onces
yon	yonder
yut	yet

Acknowledgements

I owe many thanks to Mr W.E. Swale, a wonderful person and family friend, who in his ninetieth year found time to pay a visit to Guide's Farm and suggested I should write this book. Very many thanks, Eric.

I am also indebted to Mr Hugh Cavendish, of Holker Hall, Cark-in-Cartmel, who so kindly wrote the foreword for the book.

Personal thanks to Mrs E.R. Williams for long and enduring patience in carefully reading through the manuscript and, from my scribble, making an excellent job of the first typescript.

My thanks are also due to Mr Tom Andrews, for the piece on the Lakeland Rose Show; Mr W.J. Benson, for helpful information; Mr J.H. Brown, for notes on the cross-bay swim; Mr and Mrs Gordon Cilgram, for information on natural history; Mr and Mrs D. Cooper, for helping out with copies of the typescript; Mr D.G. Harrison, the local Sea Fishery Officer; Mr John Heath, for his helpful suggestions; Mr Leonard Howe, for encouragement in the early stages; the Rev Geoffrey Howerd, for information on the desert wheelbarrow; Miss Linda Lawrence, who painstakingly typed the final draft; Mr Hugh Rom, Terresearch Ltd, for his approval of chapter 9, 'The Morecambe Bay Barrage Survey'; Mr Vernon Sandeford, who first suggested that I should approach David & Charles, the publishers; and to David & Charles themselves, and Miss Frances Head, assistant editor, for their courtesy and consideration. If I have inadvertently left out anyone among the many friends and acquaintances who gave me help, I hope they will accept my apologies; they are nevertheless included in my thanks.

I am most grateful to everyone who provided me with photographs. I am only sorry that it was not possible to use them all; for those which have been reproduced, acknowledgements are due to the following: Granada Television (4, 5, 6); Mr Sid Little (8); Mr David Longmire (7, 9); the *North-Western Evening Mail* (10, 11, 13); Mr Raymond Sankey (3); Terresearch Ltd (12); and Mrs Ethel Tyson (1, 2). The map of the barrage survey was drawn from Water Resources Board drawing 3926/C2/1 (Crown Copyright), kindly provided by the Hydraulics Research Station, Wallingford.

Finally, I would like to thank my family, and especially my wife Olive, for all their help and patience during the writing of the book. I particularly appreciate Olive's drawings which have been used to illustrate the text.